4x4

A Practical Guide to Off-Road
Adventures in Southern Africa

In fond memory of my grandfather and Namibian
pioneer, Abraham Albertus Erasmus (1895–1976), who gave
me my first lessons in a 4x4 and instilled in me
a love for the African veld.

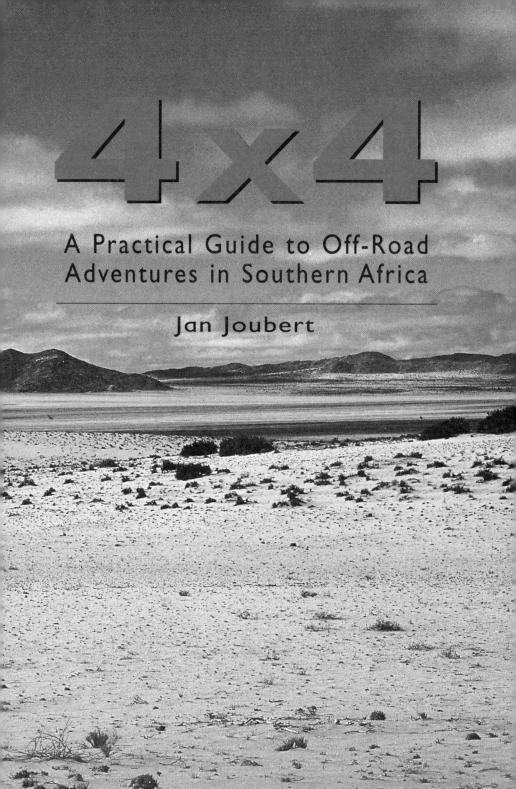

4x4

A Practical Guide to Off-Road
Adventures in Southern Africa

Jan Joubert

Struik Publishers (Pty) Ltd
(a member of Struik New Holland Publishing (Pty) Ltd)
Cornelis Struik House
80 McKenzie Street
Cape Town 8001

Reg. No.: 54/00965/07

First published in 1999

2 4 6 8 10 9 7 5 3 1

Managing editor: Annlerie van Rooyen
Editor: Alfred LeMaitre
Editorial assistant: Cara Cilliers
Design manager: Janice Evans
Designers: Dominic Robson and Sonia Hedenskog-de Villiers
Picture research: Carmen Watts and Cara Cilliers
Cartographer: John Hall
Illustrator: Clarence Clarke
Indexer and proofreader: Lesley Hay-Whitton

Reproduction: Hirt & Carter Cape (Pty) Ltd
Printed and bound by National Book Printers,
Drukkerystreet, Goodwood, Western Cape

ISBN 1 86872 173 6

FRONT COVER: *Convoy in the Kaudom Game Reserve, Namibia.*
BACK COVER: *Land Rover on the Hex River 4x4 Trail, Western Cape.*
SPINE: *4x4 on the Sani Pass, Lesotho.*
TITLE PAGE: *Land Rover in the Namib Desert, Namibia.*

CONTENTS

PREFACE

No man can live this life and emerge unchanged.
He will carry the imprint of the desert, the brand which marks the nomad;
and he will have the yearning to return. For this cruel land can cast a spell which
no temperate climate can match.

Wilfred Thesiger, explorer

After the successful publication of my booklet on 4x4 routes in Namibia in 1997, I received many calls from people urging me to make available a more comprehensive guide for the off-roader. I hope to fulfil the need for such a guide with this book and, in so doing, share the difficulties and pleasures that I have experienced during almost a lifetime in the veld. I hope I will be able to spare you some of the more unpleasant experiences, although you will probably encounter your own difficulties. Try to prepare for them, and view them as challenges.

Over the years, I have been humbled many a time by the power of nature and the fallibility of man-made equipment. This has not lessened my deep, abiding love for the African bush, but has rather increased my understanding of the awesomeness of our Creator. Moreover, it has spurred me on to investigate every nook and cranny for better products and more effective ways of off-roading. Therefore, forgive me if I seem to criticise certain products, but everything I recommend in this guide has been proved the hard way and is not simply based on sales talk or company publicity.

This book presupposes that you have some basic technical knowledge of motor vehicles. I recommend that you read the book before embarking on a 4x4 adventure, as it sets out everything that you need to know when preparing for a trip. However, it should prove equally handy during the tour, as it offers advice which you may only be able to use once you are in the bush. I trust that your whole family will read it and, if you are travelling in a group, that it will be passed around to everybody. It is is my sincere hope that *4x4 – A Practical Guide to Off-Road Adventures in Southern Africa* will contribute towards a trouble-free and enjoyable time in the veld.

Jan Joubert

1

ENJOYING NATURE TO THE FULL

Embarking on a 4x4 journey is always an adventure and a challenge. To make the experience really memorable, however, you should take the time to observe and enjoy the natural world around you. Many novice off-roaders spend their first trip worrying about and fidgeting with equipment, or else are so charged with excitement that they do not take much notice of their surroundings. After a few trips, though, most off-roaders find that such feelings diminish, and the enjoyment of nature and other people on the tour increases.

Understandably, it takes time to make a complete break from the ready-made and immediate pleasures that civilisation has to offer. As these pleasures are not available in the veld, many people try to compensate for them by partying late into the night. In order for us to appreciate nature,

however, we need to learn to keep quiet, to listen, to look and to smell.

I suggest you choose a specific subject to study and observe while you are in the veld, whether it be birds or bird calls, wildlife photography or the identification of plants (especially flowers and trees), insects or animal tracks. Stargazing is another wonderful pastime and something well worth doing as the stars are so clearly visible in the veld. Start with a particular subject that interests you and you will go on to explore related issues. Ask yourself questions such as: 'Why does the Waterberg Plateau Park have over 200 species of bird? Is it because four biomes exist there in close proximity to each other, with each biome supporting its own particular species of birds? Which plants and trees occurring in these biomes bring about this specialisation of bird species? What other animals are bound to these biomes? Which predators live there?'

A good starting point is to invest in a pair of binoculars and a field guide to birds, trees or mammals. These will help you to observe nature in its fullness.

CONSERVATION

I would like to take this opportunity to urge Southern African off-roaders to become more closely involved in conservation issues. After all, apart from the fun of off-roading, the enjoyment of nature is the core issue. Therefore, I strongly advise you to join an off-roading club. Over the years, I have corresponded with several such clubs and have been deeply impressed by their extremely high ethical standards.

Off-roading clubs should register their organisations, or at least make themselves known to official conservation agencies and NGOs. There are a multitude of these bodies doing marvellous work, and I must make a heartfelt plea for a closer relationship between off-roaders and such agencies. No Southern African off-roading club should be without some kind of formal recognition from local conservation agencies.

Furthermore, I urge that clubs or individuals should become involved in at least one conservation or conservation/research project. Organised groups can make a valuable contribution in financial terms, and could also assist in many other ways – for example, by counting birds or rhino. Another tip to off-roaders is that, before entering an area, pay a courtesy call on the nature conservator or warden responsible for that area. This is a simple gesture, but one that can be of immense help to both parties; I have even seen a warden join an off-roading group – resulting in a richer, more intensive experience of the area for all concerned.

Some conservation agencies appoint 'honorary wardens', usually a person who is involved in conservation issues and whose conduct is of such a high calibre that the agency wishes to acknowledge that individual's contribution. This is very positive, and something for which clubs or individuals should strive.

ETHICS

Throughout the years, I have always been astounded by the deep gulf that exists between people who conduct off-roading in an ethical way and those who do not. People with an ethical approach do not wish to destroy or harm their surroundings. They may be seen with a bird book, softly calling out to the birds so as to observe them better. I fondly remember people like Des and Jen Bartlett, the famous nature cinematographers, who kept a broom in their 4x4 to sweep away any unnecessary tracks which they had made.

On the other hand, I have unpleasant memories of a group in Botswana who made a bonfire one evening using three enormous trees. And I recall other groups who left their camp sites looking like a municipal dump, and people in the Kruger National Park who shot at animals with catapults. These are the people who give off-roading a bad name. Their behaviour certainly justifies the strong action taken by conservation authorities, though unfortunately this also deprives the well-behaved, ethical off-roader of a pleasurable time in the bush.

With increasing numbers of foreign visitors coming to Southern Africa, the market for self-drive adventures has grown immensely.

I view this development with a certain amount of concern, for with increased numbers of people has come an increase in unethical behaviour – mainly caused by ignorance and a lack of information.

The off-road fraternity should speak out against unethical behaviour – whether caused by locals or foreigners. A friendly talk is normally sufficient, although I recall one occasion when I made a group of Italian travellers return to their camping site in Kaokoland to clean it up.

ETHICS AND CULTURE
Another sensitive aspect is that of contact with African people who still follow a traditional way of life. In the course of your travels, you will be faced with many different shades of tradition. I have a special respect for the Himba people of northern Namibia, a respect that stems from the fact that these people have successfully lived in an extremely harsh environment for a very long time. They are very proud of their way of living and jealously guard against the encroachment of Euro-centred ways.

One cold winter day, we came upon a Himba man, his torso

exposed to the elements. He begged for my T-shirt (as well as some alcohol). I was faced with a dilemma: my Christian upbringing told me the man was cold and in need, but my conscience was telling me that I would be contributing, albeit in a small way, to the destruction of his way of life. To make matters worse, I was travelling with a lovely old Dutch woman on her first trip to Africa.

This woman had brought along some Dinky toys – miniature fire engines and European cars – as presents for the Himba children. Of course, neither the Himba man nor his children had ever seen a fire engine, or, for that matter, a Dinky toy. In the end, the Himba man put on the T-shirt, drank the beer and hung the red Dinky fire engine around his neck. My Dutch friend was happy, but I was distressed by this lack of understanding.

The point is that the off-roader should always respect other cultures and, as far as possible, not do anything to change or initiate change in other cultures. It remains these peoples' right to decide exactly how and when they wish to bring about change.

ETHICAL DEVELOPMENT

This brings us to another sensitive matter: is it ethical to develop 4x4 trails, or do they contribute to the degradation of nature? As the initiator of the Kaokoland 4x4 Trail and the Kalahari–Namib 4x4 Trail, and consultant on the Namaqualand 4x4 Trail, I have had to face some severe criticism, both from 'preservationists' – usually people with vested interests to protect – but also from genuine conservationists.

In recent years, the growth in the market for 4x4 recreation has been nothing less than spectacular, and the development of more 4x4 routes – for recreational, conservation and economic reasons – is imperative. Apart from this, the taxpayer has the right to enjoy, albeit wisely, our splendid Southern African environment: Namibia, for example, has the largest declared park in Africa – the Namib–Naukluft Park – of which barely 25% is accessible to the public, who, through their taxes, must pay for an unused area as big as France.

Most conservation authorities have tackled the popularity of off-roading in a negative way – even to the extent of being aggressively opposed to off-roading. This negative attitude opened up an information gap between those who should conserve (and teach) and those who wish to utilise. It has indeed created a negative impact, and I place the blame squarely on the shoulders of those conservation agencies who refuse to come down from their ivory towers. However, I should add that most conservation agencies have changed their attitudes considerably over the last five years, with some even opening their own 4x4 routes.

There are very few road maps or information booklets to guide visitors in the do's and don'ts of how to behave once they are out in the bush. I sincerely hope that this book will help to correct this deficiency (*see* page 132).

When considering the ethics of developing a 4x4 route, the following aspects are of importance:

• The route should be developed in consultation with the community.

• The whole community (or communities), not just a few individuals, should benefit, or have the right to benefit from, the route.

• Routes should be planned so as to minimise damage to sensitive geological areas, as well as to sensitive flora or fauna. Historical sites or places of cultural importance should also be protected.

• Specific visitor amenities should be created. For example, camp sites should be supplied with basic facilities (ablutions, fire areas and refuse removal). These can be managed by local communities or by the appropriate conservation agency.

• There should be provision for eco-friendly recreational activities, for example, guided/unguided hikes, mountain-bike routes, donkey or horse-riding routes, etc.

• There should be provision made for some form of management and control of the trail.

• Sufficient information should be made available, not only on the natural aspects of the route, but also on the cultural aspects of the region and appropriate conduct for visitors. I have found that ignorance about nature often leads to unethical behaviour. I have had groups of people going on off-road trips for the status alone, with no interest in their surroundings. I have also had groups that were willing to learn about nature as I explained it and opened it up to them. It is a special moment when I see a young person after many years, and he or she remembers with fondness my lessons on trees or birds.

I speak from experience when I encourage you to learn more about nature, as you will gain a greater appreciation of the environment and a deeper understanding of your place in it.

2

PLANNING YOUR TRIP

The planning phase is vital to the success of your trip. It should never be tackled in an offhand way, as poor planning may cost you dearly in the bush. I once met a group who experienced terrible problems with their petrol vehicles on a trip from South Africa to Cairo. Due to inadequate research, they were unaware that most of the countries north of Zimbabwe do not have the same quality of petrol as is available in Southern Africa. Also victims of poor research were an elderly French couple whom I found stranded at Orupembe in Kaokoland without sufficient food, water or fuel. They were under the impression that Kaokoland has an abundance of hotels and fuel stops. The only way to avoid potentially dangerous situations like these is to plan your trip thoroughly. Here are a few pointers:

• Calculate how long it would take to reach your destination. It may take longer to get to some places than you had anticipated due to bad roads, floods or problems with the vehicles. Depending on the time of year, you will have to take weather conditions into consideration; for example, in summer, some roads may be blocked due to rivers in flood. You may need to make a stopover, so allow plenty of time for any unforeseen occurrences. Always add at least two extra days to your itinerary; these days can be used towards the end of the tour for sightseeing or relaxation once you have left the remote areas and are within reach of help should anything unexpected happen.

• You will need to establish the condition of the roads, as this will determine the average speed at which you will be able to travel. Once you have worked out your average speed, calculate the distance that you will be able to travel per day. Be sure that you allow sufficient time to pitch camp while it is still light. Obviously, you will have to be disciplined and depart on time each morning!

• Once you have an idea of the total distance that you'll be travelling, work out the amount of fuel you'll need. To do this, you first need to know the fuel consumption of your vehicle per kilometre. Remember that a fully loaded vehicle towing a trailer in off-road conditions will have a higher fuel consumption than would be the case in normal city driving, so do not use the consumption reading that your vehicle attains in the city. Check the capacity of the main and auxiliary fuel tanks, and calculate the number of jerry cans that will be needed to hold additional fuel.

• Obtain good, up-to-date topo-graphical, as well as road, maps and confirm that their information is correct by comparing them with aeronautical charts, as these are usually very accurate. Unfortunately, many of the road maps available depict incorrect or misleading infor-mation, and the same goes for some travel guides. It will undoubtedly be worth your while to go the extra mile to verify your information.

• It is extremely useful to have a Global Positioning System (GPS). When used in conjunction with 1:50 000 maps of the intended route, GPS will enable you to measure the latitude and longitude of strategic points like landmarks, water sources, possible camp sites and splits in the road. In off-road conditions, pinpointing the latter can be of critical importance, as often a track will split into several similar-looking tracks – very confusing, especially with no road signs to guide you! By making use of GPS, you will be able to plan your entire trip in detail and thereby eliminate a great deal of uncertainty (*see* page 50).

• It is particularly important to establish the location of all fuelling points and garages which offer repairs. If there are any garages situated along your route, find out for which makes of vehicle they stock spare parts. Research the whereabouts of hospitals, doctors, clinics, aerial and other medical evacuation services, and determine the location of shops so that you can stock up on food and other supplies if you run short.

• Decide which places of interest you wish to visit, and at which hotels, lodges or camps you will be staying. Most conservation areas do not allow casual visitors, and consequently you have to apply for permits in advance and pay entrance fees.

• Study all the information that is available on the area through which you will be travelling: read up about the history, the landscape, the people and their culture, and study your field guides.

• Draw up an itinerary and give a copy to a friend. If possible, keep in regular contact with this person while you are in the bush in case any emergencies arise.

SAMPLE ITINERARY
The following is an example of the kind of itinerary that you would need to draw up for a 4x4 expedition. It is important to stress that prices for fuel, food and accommodation will vary from place to place, but you could use these suggestions as the basis for almost any tour.

Eight adults are planning a 14-day safari from Cape Town to Kaokoland in Namibia and back. They will be driving two double-cab 4x4 bakkies, each with a main fuel tank of 80 litres, plus an auxiliary tank holding 65 litres. The average fuel consumption is eight kilometres per litre on tarred roads and five kilometres per litre in off-road conditions. The fuel price is R2,00 per litre to Kamanjab and R2,50 per litre in Kaokoland and Damaraland.

As mentioned previously, it is important to research your route thoroughly. The road maps used to plan this route are as follows:

• *Illustrated Road Atlas of South, Central and East Africa* (Map Studio, 1994);
• *Road Map of the Republic of Namibia 1997* (Ministry of Environment and Tourism);
• *Kaokoland Kunene Region Tourist Map* (Shell Namibia Ltd);
• *Jan Joubert's 4x4 Routes of Damaraland, Kaokoland, Bushmanland, Kaudom* (1997).

The charts that were used include *World Aeronautical Chart 1:1 000 000* (Surveys and Land Information, Mowbray, Cape Town; chart nos. 3273, 3179).

ROUTE PLANNER

Once they have drawn up a rough plan (see table on opposite page), the group holds a meeting to discuss the following issues:

• As the route planning table shows, the total distance for the trip is estimated at 5 255 kilometres, with 11 days out of 14 to be spent on the road. To drive an average of 477 kilometres per day is an unrealistic goal, particularly in off-road conditions. Since they have three spare days, the group decides to rest for a day each at Epupa Falls, Marienfluss at Otjinungwa – Van Zyl's Pass lies between Epupa Falls and Marienfluss and represents an extremely arduous stretch – and Puros, which is close to Sesfontein and Kamanjab in case vehicle repairs become necessary.

• To drive 905 kilometres in one day from Windhoek to Epupa Falls is very demanding, particularly after driving 1 500 kilometres the previous day from Cape Town. So the group decides to spend one night at Opuwo Lodge in Opuwo, the main town of Kaokoland, leaving a mere 187 kilometres to

drive the next day to reach Epupa Falls. The reason for this decision is that there are no special places of interest to visit between Windhoek and Opuwo. Spending a day in the Etosha National Park was considered as an option, but was rejected, as one day was thought to be insufficient time to see the park properly.

• The distance between Epupa Falls and Van Zyl's Pass (172 kilometres) is deceptive, and cannot be covered in one day due to the very poor condition of the route. Instead, the group plans to reach Otjitanda by sundown.

• Lengthy discussion reveals that the total distance of 5 255 kilometres is an underestimate, as it does not take into account any extra driving for game viewing. Since game viewing must be limited in accordance with the fuel that they have available for 14 days, the group decides to take enough fuel to cover a total of 5 312 kilometres, but then rounds off this figure to a total distance of 5 500 kilometres to be on the safe side; this will leave 188 kilometres to spare.

ROUTE PLANNER (TIME AVAILABLE 14 DAYS)

FROM-TO	ROAD CONDITION	DISTANCE	TIME AVAILABLE	FUEL AVAILABLE	ACCOMMODATION
CAPE TOWN TO WINDHOEK	TAR	1 500	1 DAY	YES	HOTEL
WINDHOEK TO EPUPA FALLS	TAR/DIRT	905	3 DAYS	YES	LODGE/CAMP
EPUPA TO VAN ZYL'S PASS	OFF-ROAD	172	2 DAYS	NO	CAMP
VAN ZYL'S PASS TO MARIENFLUSS	OFF-ROAD	46	1 DAY	NO	CAMP
MARIENFLUSS TO PUROS	OFF-ROAD/DIRT	247	2 DAYS	NO	CAMP
PUROS TO ONGONGO	DIRT	134	1 DAY	YES	CAMP
ONGONGO TO PALMWAG	DIRT	91	1 DAY	YES	LODGE
PALMWAG TO KHORIXAS	DIRT	217	1 DAY	YES	LODGE
KHORIXAS TO WINDHOEK	TAR	443	1 DAY	YES	HOTEL
WINDHOEK TO CAPE TOWN	TAR	1 500	1 DAY	YES	HOME
TOTAL		5 255 KM	14 DAYS		

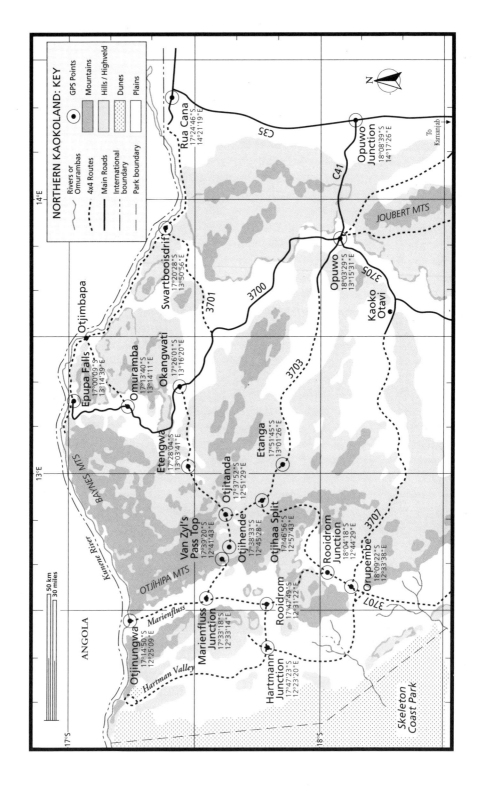

PROGRAMME

Day 1 Depart from Cape Town at 4:00 a.m. Drive northward for approximately 16 hours, directly to Windhoek.
Sleep over at Hotel Garni.
Total distance covered is 1 500 km.

Day 2 From Windhoek, drive directly to Opuwo in Kaokoland (Windhoek Otjiwarongo–Outjo–Kamanjab–Opuwo).
Spend the night at Opuwo Lodge.
Total distance covered is 718 km.

Day 3 Opuwo to Epupa Falls (Opuwo–Okangwati–Epupa).
Camp at Epupa Falls.
Total distance covered is 187 km.

Day 4 Camp at Epupa Falls.

Day 5 Epupa Falls to the Otjitanda area.
Make camp.
Total distance covered is 132 km.

Day 6 Otjitanda to Otjihende, Van Zyl's Pass, the Marienfluss.
Camp at the Kunene River at Otjinungwa.
Total distance covered is 86 km.

Day 7 Camp at Otjinungwa.
Visit rapids on the Kunene River.
Total distance covered is 17 km.

Day 8 Drive to Rooidrom, Orupembe, Kumib River and Puros. Camp.
Total distance covered is 247 km.

Day 9 Scout Puros area for wildlife.
Total distance covered is 40 km.

Day 10 Puros via Giribis Plain to Sesfontein. First fuel stop.
Camp at Ongongo.
Total distance covered is 134 km.

Day 11 Ongongo to Palmwag.
Sleep over at Palmwag Lodge.
Total distance covered is 91 km.

Day 12 South to Twyfelfontein, Petrified Forest and Khorixas.
Sleep over at Khorixas Lodge.
Total distance covered is 217 km.

Day 13 Khorixas to Windhoek.
Total distance covered is 443 km.

Day 14 Windhoek to Cape Town.
Total distance covered is 1 500 km.

BUDGET

Fuel (for 2 vehicles):

on tar: 8 km/l for 5 000 km @ R2.00 per litre	R2 500.00
off-road: 5 km per litre for 500 km @ R2.50 per litre	R500.00

Accommodation (for 8 people):

Windhoek (*Hotel Garni*) x 2 nights (dinner, bed and breakfast) @ R200 per person	R3 200.00
Opuwo Lodge x 1 day (dinner, bed and breakfast) @ R240 per person	R1 920.00
Camping at Epupa Falls x 2 days @ R20 per person	R320.00
Camping at Otjinungwa x 2 days @ R20 per person	R320.00
Camping at Puros x 2 days @ R20 per person	R320.00
Camping at Ongongo x 1 day @ R20 per person	R160.00
Palmwag Lodge x 1 day (bed and breakfast) @ R140 per person (excludes R40 per person à la carte supper)	R1 440.00
Khorixas Lodge x 1 day (dinner, bed and breakfast) @ R160 per person	R1 280.00

Food and beverages:

Food @ R30 per person per day:	R3 360.00
Beverages @ R30 per person per day:	R3 360.00

Tips and miscellaneous payments:	R300.00
Entrance fees (where applicable):	R350.00

Emergency kitty @ R1 000.00 each (refundable):	R8 000.00

Total cost:	R27 330.00
Cost pp:	R3 416.25
Less emergency kitty (refunded):	R1 000.00

Total cost pp:	R2 416.25
Cost per pp per day:	R172.59

Provided that no emergencies or other unforseen events, it would cost each person R172.59 per day to go on this 4x4 trip. You could argue that hidden expenses, such as servicing your vehicle and replacing worn tyres, might negate this figure. Even so, off-roading is still one of the best ways for a family or small group to explore and enjoy the countryside at a reasonable cost. Spread your costs over time and slowly build up your stock of camping equipment, spare tyres and other necessities. In the above example, the group's expenses could be drastically reduced by avoiding hotels and lodges, and camping wherever possible.

CO-ORDINATING A GROUP

If there will be more than one vehicle on a tour, all the members of the group should get together beforehand in order to co-ordinate the purchasing and packing of food, equipment, spare parts and tools (*see* page 92).

• *Food*: It is always a good idea to work out a menu before you leave, and to buy food after taking the whole group's needs (and tastes)

into account. One vehicle could carry the breakfast items, another vehicle the lunch, and so on.

• *Equipment*: One of the vehicles on the tour could be fitted out for carrying the fuel or the fridges, particularly if someone is driving a single-cab bakkie. However, this person's luggage will then have to be carried in another vehicle to prevent overloading. If there is a large group, and one vehicle is acting as a 'fuel bowser', then special arrangements may be needed to prevent fuel drums from rolling around. Depending on the type of vehicle involved, it may be necessary to have special brackets made for this purpose.

• *Spare parts*: It would be ideal if all the vehicles on the tour were manufactured by the same company. Then you would only need to carry one set of spare parts for the whole group. But, if there are different makes involved, spare parts should be carried for each one.

• *Tools*: To cut down on space and weight, take only one high-lift jack and one full set of spanners.

3

YOUR VEHICLE

I remember the arguments we used to have, as children, over the pros and cons of a Chevrolet versus a Ford. However, in this chapter I do not wish to become embroiled in the arguments over which vehicle to choose.

The 4x4 market has grown dramatically in recent years, and there is now a tremendous range of vehicles available. The following is a broad aid to help you in your choice of vehicle and equipment.

First and foremost, your choice of 4x4 vehicle will inevitably be dictated by cost. In this respect, the pricing of the vehicle is important, but remember that most 4x4 vehicles have a very high resale value. Be sure that you compare costs on service and spare parts, as both will be decisive factors in your success as an off-roader.

It is important to consider for which purpose you will use your vehicle and the terrain that you intend to cover. Moderate terrain (gravel roads, some off-roading, requiring intermittent use of 4x4 mode) and weekend use may call for a smaller vehicle with less space. If you are going to travel long distances and cover serious terrain (bad roads, with low range and diff locks required), then a medium to large vehicle will be required.

Naturally, the size of your family will influence your choice of vehicle. A smaller vehicle with less leg space in the back may do while the children are still small, but teenagers need as much space as grown-ups.

There is a tendency on the part of manufacturers to cram their vehicles with a lot of luxury appointments. Cup-holders or a fancy air conditioner certainly add to your comfort, but will not necessarily improve the performance of your vehicle or help you to survive in the bush. You should avoid too many extra features of this kind, and let practicality be your guide.

By the same token, I simply do not trust highly technical automotive engineering, such as computer-controlled engines and intercoolers. I have grudgingly accepted turbo in diesels, but only after a cooling mechanism became available that cools the turbo after switching off. Before that, I saw all too often what happened when turbos packed up in the middle of nowhere.

It may sound as if I'm harking back to the good old days, when the 4-cylinder Land Rover – with its all-metal dashboard and distinctive yellow and red gear knobs – was about all that was available. I realise that engine design, road-holding ability and safety features have all been greatly improved over the years, but I prefer simplicity, and become irritated with gadgets that are likely only to give problems and merely serve to push up the price.

The 4x4 vehicle has changed from a pure workhorse into what is now known as the 'recreational vehicle'. This, of course, has entailed many improvements intended to make driving a pleasure and not merely a job. The pure workhorses still remain, mostly in the form of single-cab bakkies.

With the increasing popularity of 4x4 recreational vehicles, just about every major manufacturer has entered the fray. There are many new names coming onto the market – particularly from Asia – and I am astonished by the quality of most of them. It is certainly no longer the farmer or forester who is the sole user of 4x4 vehicles.

Unfortunately, it is also true that some of these new vehicles are simply not fit to tackle the African bush. Many of them seem to be aimed more at the 'status market' than the true off-roader. By the same token, some of these vehicles have become so luxurious and pricey that their owners simply refuse to take them on safari. Are you willing to submit your R250 000 vehicle to the scratching and pounding it will endure in the veld? I think the answer is self-evident.

THE BASICS

When deciding on a 4x4 vehicle, don't be dazzled by all the extra features available. Consider the following aspects as well:

• *Fuel consumption*: The figure for fuel consumption in off-road conditions is sometimes difficult to find, as most motoring magazines give an average on tarred roads. However, there is a reason for this, as most 4x4s will spend 80–90% of their time in towns and cities. However, if a vehicle uses an excessive amount fuel in off-road conditions, this will certainly limit its usefulness. Diesel vehicles, when compared with petrol-driven ones, traditionally have a very low rate of fuel consumption. The advent of turbos and intercoolers for diesels has changed the image of diesels as smoky, noisy and smelly. However, the cost of these innovations has dramatically boosted prices.

• *The approach and departure angle*: This refers to the angle at which a vehicle can ascend (and ascend after a dip) without suffering damage to either the front or the back. One tends to forget that some vehicles have a high degree of approach angle, but when going through a severe dip, the back of the vehicle may be damaged. On average, both angles should not be less than 35°, as measured between the wheel and the lowest point (normally the bumper) in the front or the back.

• *Ground clearance*: Your vehicle's differentials should be *at least* 215 millimetres above the ground. In remote places like Kaokoland, lower-slung vehicles are regularly damaged by flying stones and rocks, especially in cases where the owner has deviated from the prescribed tyres and rims, thereby reducing ground clearance even further. In Botswana, with its notorious *middelmannetjies* (the hump between two wheel tracks), you will sometimes see the marks of a vehicle's differential in front of you for many kilometres, eventually changing to a telltale ribbon of oil.

• *Gradient*: This is the angle at which a vehicle can climb. Under normal circumstances, your vehicle should be able to tackle a gradient of at least 30° in low range and 15° in high range.

• *Roll-over gradient*: This is the angle at which a vehicle can stand before toppling over sideways. Without roof carriers or anything on top to disturb this factor, the roll-over gradient should be a minimum of 30°. A light aluminium roof carrier will not greatly change your vehicle's roll-over gradient. However, loading the roof carrier with heavy objects, such as water or fuel cans, could have a negative impact.

• *Availability of spare parts*: It is no use tackling an extended tour from the Cape to Cairo if there will be no spare parts and service facilities available along your route. The availability of spares is a very real and limiting factor for those wishing to embark on extended tours.

• *Protection under the vehicle*: To what extent are the sump, drive train and fuel tank protected? In my book, the more under-vehicle protection you have, the better off you will be.

• *Degree of sophistication of the engine*: Be wary of highly sophisticated engines. A simple but efficient engine may not be quite as fast or deliver as much torque, but neither will it require special equipment or computer analysis in the event of a breakdown. The worst scenario for the off-roader is a computer chip that fails in the deep bundu.

DIFFERENT CLASSES
What follows is a brief survey of the different types of 4x4 vehicles. Each class of vehicle has been rated according to the Kaoko Scale, (*see* box below) a rating system I devised for the first 4x4 routes in Namibia. We were looking for a way to simplify the conditions the off-roader is likely to encounter. Each class of vehicle has been rated according to the range of conditions and terrain it can handle.

The Kaoko Scale
1 = Good road, no 4x4 needed;
2 = 4x4 mode needed intermittently (moderate terrain);
3 = Difficult road, 4x4 mode needed permanently (moderate to serious terrain); (**3+** = applicable to certain vehicles only);
4 = Bad road, low range and diff locks needed (serious terrain): (**4+** = Go-anywhere capability; applicable to certain vehicles only).

The Small Recreational Vehicle (RV): *Toyota RAV4, Suzuki, Land Rover Freelander, Daihatsu, Honda CR-V, Kia, etc.*

These beautifully appointed 'fun' vehicles are intended mostly for city driving, but also for light to moderate off-roading. They perform well on tarred roads and are excellent on graded dirt roads – even in muddy conditions.

The small RVs should not be used in difficult terrain, though, as they are too low. With the addition of a small trailer, these vehicles are good for weekend getaways.

Kaoko Scale rating: 1–2

The Short Wheelbase (SWB): *Mitsubishi, Land Rover, Toyota SWB models.*

These vehicles can muster as much power as long-wheelbase vehicles (medium-sized 4x4s and larger). For instance, the SWB Land Rover is legendary as a dune vehicle in the deep Namib Desert: it is lighter than its longer cousins, and the short wheelbase gives it a better angle of attack on gradients.

The SWB vehicles have very little cargo space, however, making the use of trailers and roof carriers a must on extended trips.

Kaoko Scale rating: 1–4+

The Medium-Sized 4x4: *Land Rover Discovery, Jeep Cherokee, Ssangyong, Mitsubishi Pajero, etc.*

These vehicles are in the serious off-road category and are aimed at the luxury market, but their off-road performances vary widely. Some, like the Land Rover Discovery, can be used in the worst terrain, while other makes are ill-suited to such treatment. Whatever their off-road performances, the luxuriousness of the medium-sized 4x4 remains a prohibitive factor; few drivers wish to expose a very expensive vehicle to the punishment of the bundu. Space is a problem, since their load areas are generally inadequate, a factor that dictates the use of trailers for extended trips.

Kaoko Scale rating: 1–3 (1–4 for certain vehicles)

The Full-Sized 4x4: *Land Rover Defender, Mitsubishi Pajero, Mercedes-Benz Geländewagen, Nissan Patrol, Isuzu Trooper, Toyota Land Cruiser, etc.*

These are purpose-built off-road vehicles with go-anywhere capabilities and space for extended trips.

Someone once described this class of vehicle as an 'iron fist in a velvet glove'. I have worked with most of these machines in bad conditions, and fully support this assessment. Unfortunately, it is difficult to attach a roof carrier to some of these vehicles, a fact which can pose a problem for longer trips.

Kaoko Scale rating: 1–4+

The Double-Cab Bakkies: *Toyota Raider, Land Rover, Ford, Mazda, Isuzu, Nissan, Colt.*

This represents the most popular category of 4x4 vehicle. The reasons are good off-road capabilities, fair pricing, good servicing and ready availability of spare parts.

However, some of these vehicles remain nothing more than a basic 'bakkie' that has been revamped. Most of them need a serious re-think of their suspension outlay, as this has a great effect on road-holding ability. In the past, the suspension of certain double-cab bakkies was so poor that some of

these vehicles totally collapsed in places like Kaokoland.

Kaoko Scale rating: 1–3+
(Land Rover 1–4+)

The Heavies: *Mercedes-Benz Unimog types, Samil 20, MAN, etc.*

These are all superior, truck-size off-road vehicles that you can kit out to cross the continent in style. The only problem with this category is that they don't fit in most of the normal car-size tracks, but that will not stop them. Their greater width, though, can pose problems when negotiating narrow gaps or bridges.

Kaoko Scale rating: 1–4

PETROL OR DIESEL?
If you are planning to embark on an extended trip to Egypt through East Africa, it is advisable to opt for diesel, as petrol is often not available, of a poor quality or lacking in the additives to which engines in Southern Africa are tuned. Diesels are more economical in terms of fuel consumption. On the other hand, if you are going to drive around Southern Africa – South Africa, Namibia, Zambia,

Zimbabwe or Botswana – then either petrol or diesel is fine.

If you buy a standard diesel vehicle, you should change your approach to driving. A diesel is not fast and has limited revolutions. It usually has immense torque at low revs, but you have to be patient.

The latest diesel innovations, such as turbos and intercoolers, are amazing in terms of both engine performance and fuel consumption. Whether they can endure serious off-roading remains to be seen.

An area of concern stems from the fact that many new 4x4 vehicles run only on lead-free petrol – a real problem when contemplating a trip to remote areas like Kaokoland and Botswana. If you are in this position, you will have to make an arrangement to carry the necessary fuel

My personal preference for uncomplicated petrol engines is based on the following:

• If a diesel develops a problem in the deep bush, then you have a serious problem on your hands.

• In my experience, anything that is added on, or fancy, raises the likelihood of mechanical problems.

• On some makes, diesels with turbos and intercoolers are more expensive than their petrol-driven stablemates. The extra cost of these features is built into the price, so you would have to drive up to 50 000 kilometres before your diesel vehicle would be comparable in value to an ordinary (and cheaper) petrol-driven 4x4.

• With a basic knowledge of petrol engines – and I recommend training in this area – you could do most repairs yourself in the bush.

THE SUSPENSION SYSTEM

When you are buying a 4x4 for regular use in the bush, you will need to decide whether the vehicle's suspension system should be fitted with leaf or coil springs.

There is no doubt that both leaf and coil springs perform well. In the past, the leaf spring has been more reliable, and of a better quality, than the coil spring, but the latter has become equally reliable, with some manufacturers recently changing from leaf to coil springs. In station-wagons, for example, this change was probably implemented to enhance the comfort of the ride.

Both systems are good enough for the most arduous terrain, but you should be aware of the following:

• The coil spring gives a smoother, softer ride than the leaf spring. Coupled with free-moving or independent axles, coil springs allow for a long up-and-down movement which stabilises the vehicle under adverse conditions. The body is kept level, which makes for easier driving.

• The smoother and softer ride provided by coil springs also hides the hammering that is sustained by the suspension. A smoother ride could encourage faster driving on bad roads, increasing the likelihood of component or tyre damage. Leaf springs, on the other hand, force people to slow down, resulting in longer component life.

• Coil springs very seldom snap, whereas leaf springs are more prone to this. Much depends on the vehicle's load and the type of terrain, but the fact remains that leaf springs tend to break more easily.

• Many 4x4 owners are unaware that the bushes on leaf springs will wear out with time. However, these days, you can buy nylon or PVC bushes which last much longer than rubber bushes.

Sometimes, due to the terrain and the load the vehicle has to carry, it becomes necessary to strengthen your vehicle's suspension by adding another blade to the existing ones. This inevitably results in a bumpier ride, especially if you are carrying a smaller mass.

An alternative is to fit a special rubber ball between the axle and the chassis; the ball acts as an auxiliary blade and shock absorber. Before going on the trip, this ball can be pumped up according to the mass that the vehicle will be carrying. This works well, and enhances the stability of the vehicle. Before you implement this system, though, pay special attention to the housing into which the rubber ball fits. This component, I believe, was designed for vehicles travelling on normal graded and tar roads. Consequently, the ball tends to slip out of its housing when driving in serious 4x4 country. If the housing is strengthened by a professional, this system will definitely enhance the suspension of your vehicle.

Another recent innovation for leaf-sprung vehicles is a type of strong spring that sits between the bush housing and the axle. This simple attachment connects these two points and pulls up the front end of your leaf spring to give it more firmness. But, unlike the extra blade, this spring does not strengthen the system. This impression of strength could lead you to overload your vehicle, and cause the leaf spring to break much sooner when off-roading, with dire consequences for you and your companions. This gadget works well on good and moderate roads.

• *A final tip on leaf springs*: If one of the springs on your 4x4 ever breaks, nearby farms, towns or mines (if any) often have welding equipment that you can use to effect repairs. Do not weld the two broken ends together in a straight line across the break, as it could easily break again. First, cut out a diamond-shaped piece from another old spring – a little advance preparation really pays off in this situation – then grind out a diamond shape on your broken spring. Weld the diamond-shaped piece into place, and then

cover the newly welded spring with sand for an hour to cool it. If you are planning a very long trip, it is advisable to carry at least one spare leaf spring.

• *Shock absorbers*: A crucial part of your vehicle's suspension system is its shock absorbers. These do not enhance the carrying capacity of your vehicle; they simply absorb the road shock from the wheels and pull the vehicle down when it jumps. In the process, shock absorbers eliminate the rapid up-and-down movement of the vehicle's body, as well as its pitching and rolling movement. This contributes to better vehicle stability and a smoother ride.

There are three types of shock absorbers: oil-filled, gas-filled and an oil-gas combination. Whichever type you choose, it is important to obtain off-road shocks. Do not even consider using other types, such as those which can be inflated. Your best option is to use the ones that were supplied with the vehicle, as these have been strenuously tested under all kinds of conditions.

Although improved shock absorbers (especially gas-filled ones) are available on the Southern African market, they are expensive and I doubt whether they will give you better performance in the long run and so warrant the extra cost. Gas-filled shock absorbers do provide a softer ride, but this could encourage drivers to drive too fast on corrugated roads, with the result that the gas becomes superheated and the seals blow. You could argue that a softer ride promotes faster driving, but bear in mind that this could lead to component damage.

Finally, a few more points about shocks and springs:

• Have the shocks and springs thoroughly checked before a trip.

• Cover the bottom end of the shocks with a piece of PVC water pipe, about 10–15 centimetres in length, so as to prevent damage from flying stones.

• Carry at least one front and rear shock as spares.

WHICH TYRES?
Practically all tyre brands are of good quality, and are the product of a great deal of research. Although

it is fashionable to be seen in a 4x4 with a neat set of broad tyres, commonly known as 'fat tackies', these soon lose their appeal when a vehicle is put through the strenuous test of off-roading. Your choice of tyres should be guided not by visual appeal but by the kinds of surfaces that you are going to traverse.

At one time, Continental's attractive RV180 tyre was the off-road flagship of this company's product range. The RV180 is a broad radial-ply tyre, with soft sidewalls, which does not withstand merciless rocky terrain. Some time ago in Kaokoland, I came across a desperate guy with no fewer than 21 punctures in his RV180 tyres! This tyre is wonderful for use on sand, though, and will give good mileage on average.

Ever since the manufacturers of medium-sized 4x4 bakkies became aware of the road-holding problems of these vehicles, they have tried to fit them with broader, radial-ply tyres. The broader tyre, without question, enhances the general road-holding capabilities of these vehicles, but certainly does not cover up glaring developmental or engineering mistakes.

Choosing the most suitable tyres is quite simple: for hard, rocky, terrain, use 6–8 cross-ply tyres (commonly known as 'bakkie tyres' in Southern Africa); for sand or mud, use radial-ply tyres. Having said that, cross-ply tyres can also be used in sand. I often drive down the soft sands of river systems in Namibia using these tyres, which I deflate to 0.8 bar in the front and 1.0 bar at the back. If you do this, do not exceed a speed of 40 kilometres per hour. The radial-ply tyre is, without doubt, superior to the cross-ply in sand or mud, and the round-shouldered ones are even better than those with a sharp-edged shoulder, especially in sand.

Bear in mind these additional points before you decide which tyres to buy:

• Cross-ply tyres tend to run hotter than radials, especially if they have not been correctly inflated. The way to check this is to do the hand test: if the tyre is very hot to the touch after a long drive, then it is under-inflated; if the tyre remains cold, then it is over-inflated. Under normal driving conditions, the tyre should be lukewarm.

• Cross-ply tyres are manufactured from a harder rubber, and the arrangement of the plies across the width of the tyre makes the side-walls very firm; cross-plies hardly ever bulge. This is a real asset in rocky terrain, where most tyre damage occurs – usually when sharp stones penetrate the sidewalls. Radial-ply tyres have soft sidewalls that are easily pierced by stones, which normally damages the tyre beyond repair.

• There is a misconception that rocky terrain can be tackled with radials that have been inflated to 4.0 bar or more. This is extremely dangerous and could have disastrous consequences: if a stone penetrates the sidewall of a radial that has been inflated to such a high pressure, then the tyre could explode. Some radials are said to handle rocky terrain very well, particularly Dunlop's Qualifier, which has a firmer sidewall. However, all radials sustain some damage on rocky terrain, as holes are gouged out of the tyre's running surface. This happens because softer rubber is used for radials; when the tyre surface hits the road at great force, the steel belt foundation does not give way, but the rubber does.

• In sandy conditions, tyres with less aggressive lugs – in other words, those without deep channels or grooves – are better, as the channels make the tyre burrow more easily into the sand. For mud, however, the more aggressive lug affords better traction.

• Another question that regularly arises about radials is whether or not they need inner tubes. Many times I have travelled through the Namib's Sperrgebiet – where the highest dunes in the world are found – with a set of tubeless radials on a broader rim, deflated to 0.6 bar in the front and 0.9 bar at the back. They stuck to the rim like magnets and I never experienced any sudden loss of pressure – but then I did drive very slowly. Using inner tubes is a personal choice, but follow the manufacturer's advice and drive slowly when the tyres are deflated.

A Legend in the Namib

Ernst Karlowa, nature conservator extraordinaire in the Namib Park (before the 'Naukluft' was added to the park name), was one of those gifted people who could 'read' the sand dunes: he knew exactly where and how to tackle these treacherous, shifting formations.

He often ventured far out into the Namib dunes in a 2x4 Ford bakkie supplied by the then South West Africa Administration. Remarkably, he used normal cross-ply tyres – the proverbial 'Marie biscuits' – that had lost their surface and been worn completely smooth.

One of his understudies later told me that Ernst believed that the lugs on ordinary tyres acted much like a *bakkiespomp*, or water wheel, quickly burrowing the vehicle deeper and deeper into the sand. Ernst demon-strated that smooth tyres – without aggressive lugs – are actually the best for driving on sand, and that tyre pressure is of immense importance: the vehicle should 'float' on the sand. Most important for the off-roader, though, is the ability to 'read' the terrain up ahead, something which requires great concentration.

4

KITTING OUT
YOUR VEHICLE

A well-equipped vehicle makes your journey pleasurable, and ensures the safety of the passengers. Most 4x4 vehicles are fitted with gadgets for your comfort and safety, and this chapter covers a few items you should not be without.

A note of warning: The off-roader is constantly challenged by the problem of what to take and what to leave, to help keep the mass down. The issue is quite simple: the heavier your vehicle is when loaded, the greater the chances of damaging the suspension, the higher your fuel consumption and the more likely it is that you will get stuck. The equipment you choose to take with you in the vehicle should accord with the expected terrain, the availability of help and the duration of the trip.

Some of my former colleagues in nature conservation have joked that, when tackling a difficult area, their only equipment – apart from the vehicle – consisted of a pipe and some tea bags!

THE PASSENGER AREA

• Inertia safety belts are essential and should always be worn in off-road conditions.

• Since off-roading is very dusty and dirty, washable seat covers are ideal. Once velour seat covers pick up spots and smudges, they are very difficult to clean.

• The dashboards of some vehicles are equipped with an inclinometer. This is a handy aid, as it shows the angle at which your vehicle is ascending or descending.

• If your vehicle does not have an engine oil temperature gauge, invest in one. The gauge will allow you to monitor the oil and water temperatures simultaneously. Off-road conditions can be extreme, even more so if you are pulling a trailer through the deep, thick sands of the Kalahari system. It is wise to be able to monitor both water and oil temperature, as these two cooling systems function independently of each other.

• Keep a fire extinguisher mounted on a bracket inside the vehicle so that it can be quickly removed if needed. It must be able to put out fuel and electrical fires, so do not buy the spray-can type as this contains too little fire-suppressant to control a serious fire – and all fires are serious! (*See* page 118.)

• Always keep No. 13 spanner in the glove compartment or other easily accessible place. In the event of an electrical fire, this important tool can be used to disconnect the battery quickly (*see* page 118).

THE LOADING AREA: STATION WAGON-TYPE 4X4 VEHICLES

• The loading bay (in single- and double-cab bakkies, the loading area is known as a 'loading box') should be separated from the passenger cabin by a strong net (swimming pool type) or even an expanded metal or aluminium screen. A screen is essential in mountainous terrain where goods can suddenly shift forward, posing a serious danger to passengers.

• If possible, do not store jerry cans containing extra fuel in the loading bay, but rather on the roof carrier. However, if you do not have a choice, cover the jerry cans with a cotton cloth and enclose them in a tarpaulin.

• Because items that are stored in the loading bay tend to move around with the movement of the vehicle, the loading bay's plastic or carpet coverings can become frayed or scratched. To prevent this, pack blankets between the goods and the wall of the cabin. This will also serve to keep the contents of the boxes a bit cooler. As an added benefit, you will have a supply of extra blankets available in case of cold weather.

• If you have an electrically-operated fridge or freezer, it is advisable to get an auto-electrician to install a three-pronged socket (like the household ones) in the loading bay, where it will not get damaged by other goods. Most fridges and freezers are supplied with sockets that fit into your vehicle's cigarette lighter, but these do not last.

• The loading bay can be kitted out with a light steel frame with sliding racks. This arrangement will hold the fridge and other items neatly in place. This obviously costs more money, but I have travelled with people whose vehicles were equipped in this way, and it is an absolute pleasure. Each item is packed in its own compartment, which can be slid out on rollers and locked back into place.

THE LOADING AREA: BAKKIES

The advantage of having a bakkie is that the loading box gives you a lot more space than the loading bay of a station wagon-type 4x4. Because you are not limited by the height of the vehicle's roof, you can definitely pack more items into the loading box. A further benefit is that you can choose between having a canopy or bakkie rails, both of which are effective.

CANOPIES

Adding a canopy certainly helps to protect your luggage. There are two types of canopies available: 1) the colour-impregnated, UV-stabilised, epoxy resin (or glass-fibre) canopy, and 2) the steel canopy. Both have their advantages and disadvantages, depending on your needs.

• *The glass-fibre canopy*: Colour-toned to match your vehicle, the glass-fibre canopy looks very smart, is light and cool, and prevents most dust from getting into your luggage. However, a glass-fibre canopy is not suitable for carrying items on a roof carrier as the brackets which fasten the canopy to the loading box are not made to support heavy weights.

Although there are various types of brackets available, none of them seem to be strong enough to support a roof carrier loaded with heavy items. On occasion, the canopy has become separated from the loading box because jerry cans and spare tyres were packed on top. If you do not pile a large mass on top of the canopy – a maximum of 50 kilograms, usually – you should not run into any problems.

However, if you still intend putting a roof carrier on top of a glass-fibre canopy, you will need to ensure that the canopy frame has been sufficiently strengthened. I recently installed a hefty roll bar inside the glass-fibre canopy of my Toyota Land Cruiser bakkie. To do this, I first had to drill holes through the canopy so that I could attach the roof carrier to the steel tubing of the roll bar. In effect, the roof carrier rests on the sturdy steel frame inside the canopy and not on the canopy itself.

Considering the price of such adjustments, it may be a better idea to buy a steel canopy, as these allow you to secure fuel and gas bottles, as well as other heavy items, on the roof carrier.

• **Steel canopies**: The disadvantage of buying a steel canopy is that inferior makes can be prone to rusting. Steel canopies are also considerably heavier than the glass-fibre type.

On the plus side, steel canopies are usually bolted down – unlike the clamp-on brackets that are used on glass-fibre canopies. Consequently, steel canopies seldom come loose.

• Both glass-fibre and steel canopies need to be fitted with air intakes or ports, which can be opened or closed at will, at the front and top of the canopy. These ports create a slight over-pressure within the loading box, which prevents dust from getting inside. They can be closed in rainy conditions.

• **Canvas canopies**: One other canopy that must be mentioned is the canvas-clad type. Sometimes, the canvas is stretched over a frame, and often the canopy has a steel roof with the sides and back enclosed by canvas. A canvas canopy is not ideal, though, especially in dusty conditions, and the use of canvas has really been eclipsed by the above-mentioned.

A few other points about the loading box:

• Most bakkies have hard suspensions, so it is advisable to cover the floor of the loading box with polyurethane matting or PVC blocks to lessen the shock. PVC blocks also make wonderful mats for the shower or for the entrance to your tent (*see* page 92).

• It is also advisable to have brackets or eyelets installed in the loading box. You can attach a ratchet tie-down to the brackets in order to keep your load pinned to the floor and lessen breakages.

RAILS

If your bakkie has rails instead of a canopy, you will have to cover your belongings to protect them from rain and dust. Buy a large tarpaulin and place it inside the loading box with the ends hanging over the rails. Once the vehicle has been loaded, fold the ends over your goods and tie them down using nylon rope or ratchet tie-downs. If this is done properly and the tarpaulin is large enough, no dust or rain will penetrate this covering.

In single- and double-cab bakkies fitted with rails, an extra loading area can be created by extending a platform over the cab of between 0.75 metres (for double-cabs) and 0.50 metres (for single-cabs) in length. This platform should be raised at least 10 centimetres above the roof of the cab and constructed in such a way that it cannot bend and damage the roof. For extra strength, weld gussets in each of the corners (*see* illustration below).

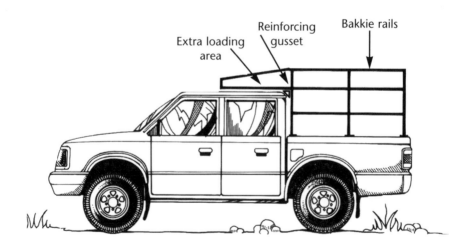

Extra loading area   Reinforcing gusset   Bakkie rails

Reinforcing gussets must be added when extending bakkie rails over the cab.

This extra loading area can be used for carrying lighter baggage.

The tailgate of the rail can be modified for easy removal and used as a kitchen or scullery table. To do this, have it welded from square tubing and then covered with an expanded metal. On the inside you could weld folding legs, each held in place by a single nut.

ROOF CARRIERS

Roof carriers significantly increase the loading capacity of your vehicle, and there are many types available on the market. Roof carriers are constructed either from aluminium or mild steel tubing, but the most important aspect to consider before buying one is the way it will be fixed to the roof.

• On a Land Rover, the roof carrier's support struts or legs are fitted into the rainwater gully. Some vehicles do not have a rainwater gully, and this presented a serious problem when these vehicles appeared on the market. The problem was recently solved through the creation of brackets that clamp neatly onto the roof at the top side of the doors without damaging the doors' rubber

sealing. I have found these brackets to be sturdy and reliable.

When installing the roof carrier, take care that the foot of the supporting strut fills the channel snugly and completely when bolted down. Fill the channel with a strip of rubber before fitting in the supporting foot, as the rubber will lessen any chafing or damage that might occur. The supporting struts must be fitted so that they are directly above the support pillars of the vehicle's roof.

• Instead of a solid foot as described above, you can also use clamps to tie down the roof carrier to the rain-water gulley. Improved clamps are now available on the Southern African market. These are flared, with a broad base, which can be clamped to the rain channel and tightened down with a bolt. Again, it is important that the clamps should be placed above the vehicle's door pillars.

• *Strengthening the roof carrier:* If you are planning to load jerry cans and other heavy objects onto the roof carrier, it is advisable to add an extra strut to each of the four corners. For the back, a ladder attached to the back of the vehicle may serve as one of the extra struts, but make sure to attach another square-tubed strut to the bumper, chassis or other reinforced point on the opposing side. The front of the roof carrier should also have two extra struts attached to the vehicle's body. For Land Rovers, you can buy a do-it-yourself kit that enables you to extend the front struts to run down to the front door hinges; the struts fit under, and are supported by, the door hinges.

In single- or double-cabs with canopies, extra struts should also be added to strengthen the roof carrier. Some body shops will punch a hole through the front fender and attach the foot of the strut to a hard point inside the fender.

It is important to note that some single- or double-cab vehicles undergo a considerable amount of body twist. Manufacturers make allowances for this by not fixing the loading box to the cab, but rather to the chassis. If you then fix an inflexible roof carrier that extends over the loading box and cab, something will have to give way sooner or later. Such roof

carriers should therefore be built in two sections that are hinged to allow for body flexing.

• *Packing the roof carrier*: When packing jerry cans, the golden rule is to fasten them down tightly at the back of the vehicle, on their sides, with the cap at the top, pointing backwards.

• *Protecting your luggage*: Just as you can prevent dust and rain from damaging your luggage in the loading box of bakkies with rails, a sturdy tarpaulin can also be used to seal your luggage on the roof carrier. The tarpaulin should be placed on the roof carrier with the ends hanging over the sides at equal lengths, except for the end hanging over the nose of the vehicle, which should be longer than the one at the back. Fold over the two sides first, then the back, and finally fold the front end over the back end so that it covers the luggage completely. Tie the tarpaulin down tightly using strong nylon rope instead of ratchet tie-downs, as these tend to develop problems in dusty terrain. The rope also has a hundred and one other uses.

A Bad Moment

Some years ago, I was travelling with the late Patrick Wagner of *Getaway* magazine, who was covering the Kalahari–Namib 4x4 Trail. We were doing a stretch on the farm 'Steinveld' in the Klein Karas Mountains when the unexpected occurred. Patrick spotted a breeding pair of black eagles, and I unwittingly drove underneath a camel thorn tree, where a twig caught the cap of one of my jerry cans on the roof carrier. For some reason, I had mounted this jerry can in front, above the windscreen – going against everything I have preached. Suddenly my windscreen, as well as the bonnet of the vehicle, was awash with petrol. Needless to say, Patrick set a new world record as he snatched the fire extinguisher, and I quickly closed the cap of the jerry can. We were quite shaken by this experience.

ADDITIONAL EQUIPMENT

• *The spare wheel*: The question of where to keep the spare wheel is always a problem. The best idea is to attach it to the tailgate of the vehicle or, in the case of single- and double-cabs with rails, to the side of the rail. It is important to find the right place for the spare wheel, as it could obstruct your visibility in the side mirror.

• *Winch*: In the many years that I have been off-roading, I have seldom needed to use a winch, and have always found that a good, broad inertia-type tow rope with proper eyelets was adequate to recover my vehicle – provided that a second vehicle was available. However, it is a good idea for at least one of the vehicles travelling in a convoy to be equipped with a winch. If you are travelling alone in the bush – which I do not advise – you should definitely equip your vehicle with one. The type of winch and its pulling capacity will depend upon the mass of your vehicle when fully loaded. It is best to buy only after consultation with suppliers.

None of the winches on the market are really strong enough to pull out your vehicle if it is completely bogged down. I have seen more than one Ramsey or Warn winch burn out as a result of over-strain. You can double the pulling power of the winch by attaching an extra pulley to a tree (the modern inertia-type belts do not damage the tree); the winch cable runs through the pulley and back to the vehicle. There are some vehicles – belonging to geologists and others who have to work in difficult terrain – with an additional pulley built into the bumper of the vehicle, so that the winch cable runs through two to three pulleys. This type of arrangement gives the winch enormous torque. However, a single pulley will normally be enough to extricate your vehicle.

• *Spotlights*: Spotlights are important for navigating through the veld at night and for spotting game or other obstructions on the road ahead. On one occasion, without a road to guide me, I had no choice but to drive through the bush at night. Fortunately, the spotlights fitted under my vehicle's roof carrier lit up the long grass for 10 metres ahead. In this way, I could clearly see obstacles like aardvark holes or rocks, which could have damaged the vehicle severely. Spotlights should be mounted as high as possible on the vehicle, otherwise they will not light up the road far enough ahead to give you enough warning of obstructions or hazards.

• *Bush bar*: It is essential that your vehicle be equipped with a bush bar (also known as a bull bar). This has protected my vehicle against serious damage on two occasions: once when I hit a kudu, and another time when I was distracted and drove into a fence pole.

Some manufacturers' bush bars are really just a cosmetic aid, and I believe that aesthetics play a bigger role in their design than practicality. Some consist merely of a single A-shaped pipe on the front of the vehicle. In order to protect your vehicle properly, the bush bar should consist of horizontal as well as vertical piping, with mesh added at strategic places – for example, in front of the radiator. The bush bar should also wrap around the front of the vehicle.

Depending on where you live, you may decide to invest in stainless steel bush bars. As I live at the coast, where rust can be a problem, I prefer stainless steel, even though it is more expensive. For inland use, normal steel will do just fine.

• *Extra fuel tanks*: You should be able to travel 1 000 kilometres with the fuel that you have in the main tank, the extra fuel tank and a few jerry cans before you have to refuel. On several 4x4 routes in Southern Africa, especially those in Botswana and Namibia, you may be forced to travel up to 700 kilometres before reaching a fuel stop. Spare fuel capacity gives you peace of mind and the opportunity to do game drives at your leisure.

Your choice of auxiliary fuel tank will depend on the space that is available under your vehicle. Some vehicles have ample space for quite large-capacity tanks, while others do not. Some manufacturers, as well as certain off-road shops, have purposely designed a range of auxiliary fuel tanks to suit different makes of vehicle.

Most auxiliary fuel tanks depend on gravity, assisted by a floor-mounted valve, for the fuel to flow into the main tank. Nevertheless, it is advisable to install an extra fuel pump to pump the fuel over into the main tank. If anything happens to the main fuel pump, the spare pump will keep you going by switching the fuel lines. It is also handy to have a fuel indicator for your auxiliary tank.

A spare fuel tank should always be mounted under the vehicle's body, both for safety reasons and to improve the stability of the vehicle. Except for jerry cans, it is not advisable to keep fuel tanks on the roof carrier.

• *Mesh cover for the radiator*: No 4x4 vehicle should be without a mosquito metal mesh cover fitted to the radiator. On a Land Rover, it can be attached to the grill; on a Land Cruiser, a light frame into which the mesh is mounted can be added to the front of the radiator. Most other vehicles will use either of these methods to cover the radiator. The mesh cover effectively prevents grass seeds and insects from clogging up the orifices in the radiator.

• *Snorkel*: A snorkel is a necessity if you are planning to be constantly fording rivers or crossing swampy terrain. Apart from the Okavango, in Botswana, we do not really have that much water in Southern Africa. Most 4x4s have a fording depth of between 750 and 1 200 millimetres, depending on the position of the vehicle's air intake. However, you may sometimes have to exceed this depth; this is where a snorkel is essential, as it prevents water from getting into the engine. However, you will also have to ensure that the distributor and spark plugs have special watertight covers (this applies to petrol-driven vehicles only; diesels have no problem in this respect; *see* page 86).

Since air cleaners and the air intakes in 4x4 vehicles are situated in the engine compartment, where they are protected against excessive dust, fitting a snorkel will increase the amount of dust sucked in, especially if the snorkel does not have its own air cleaner. In very dusty conditions – which covers most Southern African off-road routes – the dust from passing vehicles is more readily sucked in if a snorkel is fitted. If you insist on having a snorkel, make sure it has its own air cleaner (like that on a farm tractor).

• *Running boards*: These have become quite popular, as they help to deflect mud and dust, and prevent stones kicked up by the front wheels from damaging the paint on the sides of the vehicle. On the one hand, I've found that running boards work just fine on vehicles such as the Toyota Raider, but that on lower-slung vehicles, like the Isuzu bakkie models, they quickly become damaged in rough, rocky terrain.

I have sometimes seen running boards that had to be removed after sustaining damage from rocks and stones. Even the side steps of a Land Rover can be damaged if you forget to pull them up before driving off.

• *Sand plates*: I have always been surprised that nobody in Southern Africa has copied the wonderful sand plates first used by German troops in the North African desert campaigns during the Second World War. (Incidentally, this is also where the term 'jerry can' was coined.) Sand plates are a real asset in sand, as well as in muddy conditions (*see* page 88). There are South African-made aluminium plates which roll up like caterpillar tracks and work quite well. I have also seen people using a type of PVC sand mat, which is useful but simply not strong enough.

At one time I used 0.5-metre ribbed drainage covers, which were efficient but very heavy. The best option is still the thick, aluminium German sand plates, which can be fixed either to the side of the vehicle or to the roof carrier. Be warned, though, that they are difficult to procure and quite costly.

• *Jack*: No off-roader should be without a high-lift jack. This can be neatly fixed to the roof carrier, bush bar or back of the vehicle. For vehicles with leaf springs, I advise taking a small bottle jack as well. This will be of great assistance if you have to replace or mend a blade. Remember that you must also carry a jacking plate (generally a stout piece of wood) so your jack will not get pushed into the ground.

An 'air jack' or 'bull bag' – which consists of a PVC bag that can be pumped up with the aid of your exhaust – is wonderful in marshy ground or deep sand. They take up very little space when deflated.

• *Jerry cans*: First, let me offer a word of warning: do not, under any circumstances, invest in PVC jerry cans. They are dangerous and

should be banned by law. In the dry, dusty climate of Southern Africa, PVC jerry cans pick up static electricity, which can be sufficient to ignite a spark during refuelling. I have seen vehicles burned out and people seriously injured when PVC jerry cans caught fire. If you do choose to carry them, at least reduce static electricity by wiping the can down with a damp cotton napkin before refuelling.

At one time, the market was flooded with cheap Chinese and Russian jerry cans. These cans were made from inferior metal that rusted easily and caused serious damage to engines because rust contaminated the fuel. It is therefore better to invest in the more expensive South African or German jerry cans. Even so, when pumping petrol or diesel over to the main tank, you should always cover the filler hose with an old nylon stocking to filter out any unwanted particles.

The lids on jerry cans have a tendency to become leaky after a while. Replace the rubber seal once a year and, in case of leaks, always carry a piece of inner tube to cover the cap before closing the lid to stop the leak. Always attend to a fuel leak! Try to buy jerry cans that have a safety pin on the cap.

• *Spare battery*: This is usually kept in the engine compartment (except in Land Rovers, where it can be placed under the front passenger seat). It is essential to have a 'deep cycle' battery as the spare, especially if you have a fridge or freezer which uses a lot of power. The benefit of this type of battery is that it can hold more electricity for longer periods of time and can be run flat several times with no ill effects. Normal car batteries seldom last if they are run flat more than three or four times. As a general rule, however, you should avoid letting any battery run flat.

The spare battery should be fitted into a sturdy bracket, which has been installed by a professional auto-electrician. A solenoid switch must also be installed; when the solenoid is on, the excess power from the main battery flows into the spare, keeping it charged. When you switch off your vehicle at the end of a day's driving, the spare battery is isolated from the main battery. This will prevent your fridge, if you have forgotten to switch it off, from drawing all the power from both the spare and main batteries. All the better if this is done automatically when you switch off the vehicle. Manual switches are available, but I do not recommend them, purely because you could easily forget to switch off the battery.

When buying a normal (i.e., not deep cycle) battery as a spare, I recommend the sealed units that are manufactured in South Africa. They are expensive, but they do last and are virtually service-free.

• *Air pump*: An air pump has a multitude of uses, apart from the obvious one of inflating tyres. It can be used for blowing open clogged fuel lines, inflating rubber ducks, blowing out dust from inside the car and even inflating air mattresses. Like the spare battery, the air pump can also be mounted in the engine compartment of your vehicle. There are several types of air pumps available. I don't recommend those which operate from the car cigarette lighter as they are noisy, overheat quickly and seize up in hot weather. The more expensive electrical unit, if installed correctly, works much better. Some types of pump are driven by the fan belt, which is very efficient and long-lasting.

You could make a very handy air pump from a small steel carbon dioxide (CO_2) bottle that can be purchased from Afrox. If you fit this bottle with a valve, you can inflate the tyres several times, and very quickly, with CO_2. When the CO_2 is depleted, you merely take it back to Afrox for a refill.

However, if you prefer to use the old manual tyre pump, rather buy the truck pump manufactured by Vetsak (and commonly known as a 'Vetsak pump'), as it has a large capacity and requires less effort to inflate a tyre.

ROOF TENTS
These tents have become very popular in Southern Africa as they are easy to erect and store, and safe from prowling wild animals and crawling insects (*see* page 92).

• The attaching brackets that hold the roof tent to the vehicle's roof should be flared and delta-shaped, as these are stronger. The frame should be made from aluminium.

• It is advisable to mount the roof tent so that it opens towards the side of the vehicle. If you mount it so that it opens towards the front of the vehicle, a boot must be welded to the bush bar (denoting, of course, that you must have a bush bar). As the ladder then sits high on the bush bar, it become difficult to climb in and out.

If you mount the roof tent so that it opens towards the back of the vehicle, it will impede access to the loading bay (or loading box). Mounting it so that it opens towards the side is the best solution, as the tent then supplies an area of shade, or even an area for ablutions.

• You can make a handy cubicle for ablutions by sticking a broad strip of Velcro to the underside of the portion of the tent that protrudes over the side of the vehicle. Cut a light, PVC canvas to size, add Velcro to the top, attach it to the tent, and you will have a private enclosure.

• It is advisable to reinforce the underside of the floors with a couple of extra channel-shaped aluminium struts (for some manufacturers' products). The folding floor is made from high-quality, marine-ply veneer, but, in the dry climate of Southern Africa, the veneer can develop cracks.

• The ladder that supports the folding half of the tent floor should be made of a thick, strong aluminium or from lightweight metal tubing. If you have to make one, construct it in such a way that the ladder's legs consist of two sections which telescope into each other and can extend for quite some length. Make holes at the bottom through which you can push sturdy pegs to support the ladder.

• Some roof tents have a single-layered, canvas roof which may leak in heavy rain. It is therefore a good idea to make a fly sheet out of UV-stabilised, PVC canvas to put over the roof when it rains. Fix it to the frame of the tent with elastic bungie cords (also known as bungies).

• Bungies can also be used to stretch over the roof tent once it has been zipped up in its carrying bag to stop the tent from flapping while you drive. Over time, the tent's waterproof carrying bag tends to stretch and become loose.

• If you have to buy a mattress, do not buy one that exceeds the suggested thickness as specified by the manufacturer. A too-thick mattress, together with bedding, makes it difficult to fold up the tent, and also stretches the tent bag. In the end, the zips will burst.

• An air-mattress is ideal to use in a roof tent, but this is the only time that I would recommend using one (*see* page 95). The downside is that you will have to inflate it every evening, but this should not be a problem if you have an electric air pump.

• Do not put a roof tent on top of a trailer, as it could easily be damaged by flying stones and grit when you are driving over gravel roads. Trailer manufacturers promote this tent-and-trailer idea as a selling point, but I do not recommend it. The exception is a roof tent that is enclosed in a glass-fibre shell. Even so, these too should be mounted as far towards the back as possible.

NAVIGATION AND COMMUNICATION AIDS

• *GPS*: A GPS (Global Positioning System) is an extremely useful navigational tool which can be used in conjunction with a map to programme your entire route. If you use 1:50 000 maps for accurate measurements, you will never get lost or be uncertain of your location again. A GPS also improves safety in that, if someone falls ill or some other problem occurs, you can radio an aeroplane or helicopter for assistance and they will be able to pinpoint your exact position using their own GPS.

The GPS unit is easily mounted in vehicles (have the work done by a professional, though) and is quick to take out and store.

• A long-distance, high-frequency radiotelephone is a very useful communications device. It once helped me in the Marienfluss Valley on the Angolan border – far away from civilisation – when the chassis broke on one of the vehicles in our convoy. Within 24 hours, we were able to re-assemble the chassis by notifying the relevant people, who flew in the necessary parts.

A radiotelephone is also great for reaching your family or friends to give them a report on your progress, or to ask advice from a doctor. Furthermore, it is useful to listen in to hear who may be bogged down by flooding rivers so that you can avoid dangerous areas.

This device is costly, and you will also need to obtain the licences necessary for the particular countries through which you intend to travel. In addition, you will have to install extra crystals for those countries that use different frequencies. Some high-frequency sets have a range of up to 1 000 kilometres in good conditions.

However, a radiotelephone is of no use if you don't know whom to contact and what procedures to follow. Most post offices have a central control station which could hook you up with telephone lines. If this facility is unavailable, you will have to tune in to the frequencies of ambulance and other backup services in the event of an emergency or breakdown.

The negative side of a radio-telephone is that, during the summer months, it will pick up any lightning that occurs within a

1 000-kilometre radius. The resulting static will make any conversation very difficult, if not impossible.

• A satellite-linked telephone represents the ultimate in modern communications devices, but it is extremely expensive. This device has built-in antennae and a GPS. Once pointed in the right direction, you can speak to someone, without interference, from anywhere in the world. You can even send faxes or e-mail using this service.

• If you are travelling in a group, I would strongly advise that you install short-distance FM mobile radios for communicating between vehicles (*see* page 122). CB radios do not serve this purpose well as they are not robust enough. It is better to use purpose-built sets that can be used in any terrain.

5

TRAILERS

The off-road trailer market has become very competitive in recent years. I remember a time when we had to chop the loading box, axle and suspension off a Toyota bakkie in order to pull heavy loads over bad terrain. Those days are long gone, and nowadays the trailers that are available in Southern Africa are well equipped to the point of being luxurious.

BUYING A TRAILER

When you are deciding on which trailer to buy, ensure that it has the following:

• Sturdy leaf springs fitted to a strong axle.

• A high-tensile steel chassis and trailing arm. Solid steel tubing is still preferable to the U-shaped iron channel which is used these days. If it is not made of extremely strong steel, the channel tends to develop cracks. I have seen some that have completely broken off.

• 750 x 16-centimetre tyres (or matched to those of the towing vehicle) and an axle width that spoors exactly with that of the towing vehicle.

• Thick, steel templates welded on top and underneath the trailing arm at the end where the female trailing coupling is fixed with high-tensile stainless steel bolts. A Trapezium-type coupling is a real asset.

• The loading box should be water- and dust-proof. A rear door that flaps downward – bakkie style – is another real asset when loading and off-loading. The loading box should have eyelets or brackets for tying down the contents.

• Brackets for holding water canisters and jerry cans should be fitted outside the trailer on either side of the wheel arches.

• The lid should fit tightly and have gas struts for easy opening and closing. If a rail has been supplied for loading equipment on top of the lid, ensure that the lid has extra supports.

• Use a universal rear light column – yellow for indicators, red for brakes. The rear lights must be clearly visible to any vehicle following, and protected or positioned so that they cannot be damaged.

• In very mountainous terrain, it is advisable to have a trailer with a brake system that is activated by the forward motion of the trailer when the towing vehicle stops.

PACKING AND SERVICING
• Pack the trailer so that it is a little heavier to the front – a load of between 100 and 150 kilograms is advisable. If your trailer is unbalanced, i.e. too little weight in front or even too much towards the back, then it will tend to lift

up the rear suspension of the towing vehicle. This increases tyre wear and can lead to poor handling of the vehicle. In the end, a wrongly packed trailer can damage the coupling, with the trailer possibly becoming unhitched.

• In very rocky terrain, secure the male–female trailer coupling with a few loops of nylon rope to prevent it from rattling, as this causes the lock in the female part of the coupling to wear out.

• Never oil or grease the trailer hook (male coupling) as it picks up grime which acts as an abrasive and wears out the coupling.

• After every off-road trip, make sure to repack the wheel bearings with grease and paint the front part of the trailer with a thick coating of rubberising paint.

TOWING A TRAILER
A well-packed and balanced trailer is a pleasure to tow. First-timers sometimes forget that they have a trailer behind them! Some people fix a broomstick with a little flag attached to the trailing arm so that

they can look in the rear-view mirror and remind themselves that the trailer is still there.

Most off-road trailers can travel at 120 kilometres per hour on good gravel or tarred roads, but this is not advisable. Depending on the make and size, a trailer packed for an extended trip can weigh up to 0.50 tonnes. This extra weight puts a heavy strain on your vehicle's brake system – most trailers are not fitted with brakes – and consequently one needs more time and distance to come to a stop. In an emergency, this can be fatal. I have seen a trailer jack-knife on a gravel road after the brakes were suddenly applied. The towing vehicle's road-holding was severely affected, and, after sliding around, it came to a halt in a cloud of dust, facing the opposite direction. The occupants were shocked but fortunately unhurt. However, the vehicle had been damaged by the trailer, and the coupling in particular was severely damaged.

Remember that a trailer is going to influence your fuel consumption on the road – but especially off the road. With a trailer in tow, your vehicle's engine must work harder, and it normally also runs hotter. I have found that long stretches of thick sand are the worst for fuel consumption and engine temperature (*see* page 37). For this reason, it is handy to have an oil temperature gauge fitted as an extra, over and above your vehicle's standard temperature gauge.

Towing a trailer over rough terrain calls for slow speed with power, so do not hesitate to go for low-range 4x4 mode when necessary. This obviously means that vehicles with trailers are slower than those without. Keep this in mind when you are travelling in a group, as it will influence the average speed of the whole group. Unfortunately, some non-towing drivers can get irritated with slower, trailer-encumbered vehicles.

Learn to 'listen' to your trailer when passing through dips and gulleys, or over rocks: you will hear and feel when your trailer's wheels have gone over or through the impediment. So don't accelerate before your trailer is in the clear.

Above all, remember that in rough terrain the movements of a trailer are going to be more severe, or pronounced, than those of the towing vehicle. If you look in your side mirrors, you'll be surprised at how much your trailer moves up and down. So keep this in mind, and reduce your speed.

• *Refrigerators*: In recent years, it has become fashionable to install fridges inside trailers. I advise the opposite: it is much better to have the fridge in the towing vehicle.

Space in the trailer is restricted, and there is no flow of air, so the pump could easily overheat – especially in summer. Apart from this, the movement of a trailer is more pronounced than that of the towing vehicle, which could lead to oil from the fridge pump entering the pump area, resulting in a blown pump. These pump units are quite expensive to replace.

6

OFF-ROAD DRIVING

Off-road driving is a skill that is acquired with time and practice. A number of off-road driving schools have been set up in major South African cities, and I urge the novice off-roader to attend a training school before tackling difficult terrain.

Although I have been driving a 4x4 for many years, I still get bogged down – although very seldom – and Van Zyl's Pass in Kaokoland never fails to make me nervous. Do not be misled by your vehicle – a powerful engine, low range and diff lock are no guarantee that you will not experience problems. Sooner or later, you will be confronted with a difficult situation that will test your abilities as an off-road driver. This is a humbling thought, but the experience will make you more alert.

Do not attempt to tackle a 4x4 route or any difficult obstacle the day that you buy your first 4x4 vehicle. Give yourself time to get to know the vehicle. Drive around on tarred roads for a couple of weeks, so that you become familiar with your vehicle and how it brakes, leans in corners, etc. For your first excursion, try the vehicle out on a steep bank or on loose sand. Take someone along who has experience of these obstacles and practise using the gear levers and diff lock. Get the feel of your 4x4 in action. The immense torque and power that the vehicle displays in the low-range mode always comes as a surprise to first-timers. Unless you are accompanied by an experienced driver, do not attempt a tough 4x4 route on your first trip.

Teach your spouse or partner how to drive the vehicle; a situation could arise when that knowledge might prove invaluable. I once met up with a couple whose brand-new

Toyota Raider was bogged down in the sand near Sossusvlei in Namibia. It was obviously their first ride in deep sand, and clearly neither of them had read the vehicle's manual: although the vehicle was in 4x4 low gear, the hub-locks had not been engaged!

The obstacles that you will face most often when off-roading are rocks, sand and mud, but you may also have to cross rivers, beaches, dunes, mountains and snow, or have to drive through very dusty conditions. When off-roading, it is important never to drive a 4x4 vehicle fast. Sustained high speed will wear out the transfer case, gearbox, differentials and engine. High speeds are also dangerous: 4x4 vehicles have a higher centre of gravity than passenger cars, and consequently roll more easily. I advise that you drive at a maximum speed of 100–110 kilometres per hour on tarred roads, 70–80 kilometres per hour on gravel roads, and at a maximum speed of 45 kilometres per hour when in four-wheel-drive mode. Always drive slowly when using more power and never charge at obstacles.

GENERAL GUIDELINES
• Always inspect an obstacle before attempting to negotiate it.

• To give you more control, keep both hands on the steering wheel in the nine-and-three position. Never hook your thumbs over the inside of the steering wheel, as a sudden jolt could break one of your fingers.

• Wear seat belts at all times (except when crossing a river), as you can be thrown around in your seat.

• When driving a vehicle with a manual gear transmission, keep your foot away from the clutch, as you could unintentionally engage it while negotiating a difficult surface.

• Before tackling a tricky situation, always select the correct gear and ratio for the surface and stick with this gear throughout.

• Ensure that your vehicle's tyres are correctly inflated.

ROCKY TERRAIN
Typical places where you are likely to encounter rocks are Van Zyl's Pass in Kaokoland (Kaoko Scale rating 4),

Richtersveld National Park (Kaoko Scale rating 3), Kunene River (Kaoko Scale rating 3), Namaqualand 4x4 route (Kaoko Scale rating 2), Kalahari–Namib 4x4 Trail (Kaoko Scale rating 2) and Matusadona and Chizarira national parks in Zimbabwe (Kaoko Scale rating 2 for both). Although you can follow clearly marked tracks in most of these places, you may sometimes have to negotiate rocky ridges and stony sections.

Rocky ground, consisting of loose stones and gravel, is the most difficult terrain on which to drive, especially if you have to ascend at a sharp angle. This is tricky as the vehicle's wheels could spin and sharp rocks puncture the tyres.

For the best results, inflate the tyres to between 2.20 and 2.50 bar at the front and between 2.50 and 3.0 bar at the back and engage 4x4 mode – high or low range, depending on the degree of difficulty. This mode spreads the torque to all four wheels instead of only the back two, ensuring longer tyre life and better control over the vehicle. Drive slowly to prevent the wheels from jumping and losing their grip, as the vehicle will need all its wheels on the ground for maximum traction. Fast driving on rocks damages the vehicle's suspension and increases the chances of a sidewall puncture.

When faced with a sharp incline, select a low gear, low range. Release the clutch and accelerate evenly, keeping your engine at a steady speed. Do not change gears until you have cleared the incline. If the vehicle starts rocking, decrease power slightly and drive even more slowly. The vehicle will seldom stall in low gear, low range and you will be surprised at how much torque is still kicked out.

Vehicles with a central diff lock, such as Land Rovers, can negotiate sharp inclines very easily. With the diff in low range, they can climb where other vehicles cannot, except on a loose gravel incline. The reason for this is that, since the vehicle pumps out incredible torque in this mode, the loose gravel could cause the wheels to spin. If this happens, decrease engine revs immediately.

SAND

Tyre pressure is the most important aspect of driving on sand. Not even the best equipped 4x4 will get through soft sand without the appropriate tyre pressure. Deflate the tyres to 0.6 bar in the front and 0.9 or 0.8 bar at the back. They can be deflated even lower without getting punctures or jumping off the rim. In effect, you are broadening the surface area of the tyre, but also lengthening the surface area that makes contact with the ground. With more rubber on the ground, it is easier for the vehicle to 'float' over the sand. Hard tyres, even broad fat tackies, will cut through the sand's crust. If you don't have a tyre gauge, use the finger method: deflate the tyres until the bottom sidewall is as wide as your index finger (*see* illustration above).

Drive at a moderate speed of about 30 kilometres per hour (terrain permitting). Do not drive

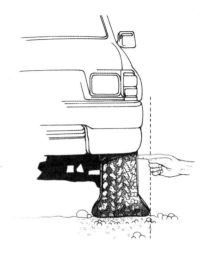

Use your finger to gauge tyre pressure.

too slowly, as you need to keep up the vehicle's momentum. The tyres will let you know if you are driving too fast: each make of vehicle reacts differently in certain conditions and you will soon get to know your own vehicle's warning signals.

The Damara tern
Smallest of all the terns, the Damara tern (*Sterna balaenarum*) breeds up to 2 kilometres inland on the Namib's gravel plains. This little bird, of which only 2 000 breeding pairs have been counted, often makes its nest in the tracks left by vehicles. The eggs, as well as the chicks, are very well camouflaged and one cannot see them from a vehicle. This is one reason why the off-roader should stay off the Namib gravel plains (*see* page 63). The other reason is that tracks left by vehicles can remain for up to 80 years.

Never use the brake to stop the vehicle, especially when driving on beaches above the high-water mark. Merely take your foot off the accelerator and depress the clutch. A small 'dune' will build up in front of both the front and back wheels, and cause the vehicle to stop. If you apply the brake, the wheels will immediately cut through the sand's crust and the vehicle will dig into the sand. When starting off again, first engage reverse gear and move backwards in your tracks for two or three paces. Then engage low gear and pull away smoothly. With enough momentum, the vehicle will be able to overcome the dune in front of its tyres.

Always keep to existing tracks or to the tracks of the vehicle in front of you. Do not sit on another vehicle's tailgate, but keep a distance of at least four or five vehicle lengths behind. The tracks can sometimes be so deep that, if the person in front of you suddenly stops, you will not be able to pass as the vehicle will remain glued to these tracks. Many vehicles have collided because people have not maintained a safe following distance. Furthermore, in the event that the front vehicle hits a bad patch of sand and gets stuck, a safe following distance allows for sufficient space for a tow rope to be attached without the second vehicle also getting stuck.

The mass of your vehicle is of critical importance (*see* page 36): the lighter the vehicle, the better it will navigate sand. In the Kalahari, I have seen a little Suzuki leave much larger Land Rovers and F250 Fords far behind.

Although sand plates are quite expensive, it is worth investing in some as they are very useful if you have to recover your vehicle from sand (*see* page 46).

DUNES

For dune driving, all the principles of sand driving apply. The difference is that on dunes you will also be ascending and descending at fairly sharp angles.

First and foremost, I would like to stress that the vehicle should always be made as light as possible, and, secondly, that nothing should be allowed that might alter the vehicle's centre of gravity – such as extra luggage or heavy items on a roof carrier.

The valley between the dunes, or the 'street', is usually the best place to drive. If you have to cross dunes, here are a few pointers:

• Remove all luggage from the roof carrier. Pack everything inside the vehicle, with the heaviest objects packed at the bottom. Ascend the dune from the windward side – the long-sloping side. Dunes mostly form sharp ridges where the windward and leeward sides meet. The windward side, which you use for your ascent, always slopes at a shallower angle to the leeward side, allowing you to ascend without rushing up the dune.

• If you do not know the route ahead, drive your vehicle to the top of the dune and let it sink into the sand: you literally 'hook' your front wheels over the ridge; your chassis normally comes to rest on the ridge. Two-thirds of the vehicle will still be on the windward slope; this mass is sufficient to allow you to reverse if needed. After inspecting the leeward angle of the dune, you either continue forward or reverse. This method is best if you have to cover a wide stretch of dunes. If you

have only one or two dunes to negotiate, you could first inspect each one on foot.

• It is not advisable to descend a dune which is steeper than 17°; in fact, an even lesser incline can be quite unnerving. Descend slowly in low gear, low range, keeping the front wheels dead straight, and accelerate slightly if you feel the back breaking away. If the incline is too steep, reverse back down the windward side of the dune.

Some dunes, such as the so-called 'barcan' dunes, also known as 'walking' dunes, which form a perfect crescent shape, and the 'star' dunes, consisting of star-shaped ridges, are sometimes impassable. Both dune types are extremely soft.

Dune driving can damage the environment in certain cases, so, where there are roads, keep to them. The coastal dunes of the southern Cape and KwaZulu-Natal in South Africa are very sensitive and are protected by law. Even where they are not protected, you should refrain from driving on them, particularly where there is some form of vegetation. Coastal dunes are important to the coastal biome and should be conserved.

The inland dunes of the Namib and Kalahari deserts can withstand greater impact as the wind quickly erases all tracks. However, there are very few opportunities for dune driving in the Namib Desert, as most of the dunes lie within conservation areas. The reason for this is not the dunes themselves, but the adjacent gravel plains, which are extremely sensitive. Large areas of these plains are covered by lichen fields. These primitive plants play a significant role in stabilising the plains against erosion, and researchers are trying to determine their significance in the food chain. The lichens depend on the fog that regularly rolls in from the cold Atlantic, and they grow extremely slowly. If you drive on them, you will destroy them, and your tracks will remain for up to 80 years.

Apart from the lichens, it is evident that the salt borne by the coastal wind reacts with the substrates of the soil, resulting in a puffy, 'lifting up' of the top layer. This process is, of course, very slow, but if you drive over the plains your vehicle will inevitably compact this layer. If the plains were open to anyone in a 4x4, the long-term results could be disastrous. Still visible along the Skeleton Coast are the tracks made by vehicles sent north from Cape Town during the Second World War to rescue survivors of the liner *Dunedin Star*, which ran aground north of Möwe Bay in November 1942.

The Kalahari Desert offers more scope for dune driving. However, by comparison to the Namib, where the dunes reach a gigantic 200 metres in height, those in the Kalahari are small, though they are nevertheless formidable.

BEACHES

The principles of sand driving also apply to driving on beaches. Normally, a beach consists of two parts: the area above the high-water mark, which is made up of deep, loose sand; and the intertidal area, which is usually a hard surface compacted by the action of the waves. Obviously, the best place to drive is the hard, flat area of the intertidal strip, as this requires relatively little effort. Even so, one should always stay alert in this zone,

The gemsbok

With the passing of the years, I have become more familiar with different species of wildlife and the wonder of creation. There is one animal for which I have special respect – the gemsbok (*Oryx gazella*). Once, we found a bull in the deep-dune Namib. This was a special moment, even for crusty old nature conservators like ourselves. As the area is devoid of vegetation or water, the animal – a superb specimen – was obviously very hardy.

The handsome gemsbok is specially adapted to survive in the harsh, if not deadly, environment of the Namib. It can tolerate body temperatures of up to 45°C, where most other animals would drop dead at 42°C. This is made possible by a marvellous internal cooling system, whereby the blood flowing to the brain is first cooled in the intricate network of blood vessels contained in the nasal passages. A gemsbok will always run into the wind when it runs away from you, as the cooler air rushing into its nostrils helps in the regulation of its internal temperature.

Apart from this, the animal's urinary and digestive systems make use of every drop of moisture that it extracts from the grass and other plants that the animal eats. Consequently, the gemsbok can go for many months, even years, without drinking.

as the viscosity of the surface may not always allow for easy driving. In many places, the sand may be soft and boggy.

I have encountered numerous shell beaches along the Atlantic coast of Southern Africa (shell beaches are uncommon along the Indian Ocean coast). This kind of surface can be difficult to cross, as the beach is made up of broken mollusc shells and is soft enough for a vehicle to sink in. If a shell beach is wet, the surface becomes even more bog-like and difficult to negotiate.

Although the public is not permitted to drive on the beach areas of Namibia's Skeleton Coast, this region – together with parts of Botswana and the Northern Cape – contains two other types of difficult terrain which should be mentioned, namely, rivers and salt pans.

PREVIOUS PAGE *A heavily
laden 4x4 convoy makes its
way through the Richtersveld,
Northern Cape.*
ABOVE *A group of vehicles
traverses the deep-dune Namib
Desert, Namibia.*
OPPOSITE *The author chats
with a group of Himba boys in
Kaokoland, Namibia.*
RIGHT *Descending the Namib
dunes calls for a steady hand.*

PREVIOUS PAGES *A trailer allows you to carry enough luggage for extended tours. This party is travelling through the Itala Game Reserve, KwaZulu-Natal.*

OPPOSITE *Negotiating a sandy stretch can require some digging – and patience!*

ABOVE *Careful inspection before crossing a river will help you to avoid getting stuck.*

BELOW *Air-jacking a Toyota 4x4, Botswana; an air jack is very effective in muddy conditions.*

PREVIOUS PAGES *When crossing a river, such as the one shown here in southern Lesotho, your vehicle builds up a bow wave. It is vital to maintain momentum in such a situation.*
ABOVE *Descending Van Zyl's Pass in Kaokoland, Namibia, calls for slow speed – with power.*
OPPOSITE TOP *The scenic West Coast presents opportunities for beach driving.*
OPPOSITE BOTTOM *The driver of this 4x4, shown in the Huanib River valley in the Namib, is too close to these elephants: always keep at least 500 metres away from these animals.*

PREVIOUS PAGES *Surveying the mighty Fish River Canyon, southern Namibia.*

OPPOSITE TOP *These Land Rovers have stopped on the Namibian side of the Orange River; the rugged Richtersveld Mountains rise in the distance across the river.*

OPPOSITE BOTTOM *Late afternoon is the time to halt and make camp. This group has parked in a laager fashion in order to afford their camp site protection from the wind.*

ABOVE *Sitting around the camp fire at sunset is one of the delights of off-roading, and gives everyone the chance to unwind after a day on the road.*

FOLLOWING PAGE *A 4x4 crosses a wooden bridge at the Kosi Forest Camp, KwaZulu-Natal.*

In the case of rivers, when the flow reaches the sea – not a regular occurrence along the Skeleton Coast – it deposits vast amounts of clay where the fresh water meets the salt water. If a strong wind is blowing, the clay may be covered by a thin layer of sand so that it resembles an ordinary beach. For the unsuspecting off-roader, this hidden quagmire can be a very unpleasant surprise.

Salt pans should in general be avoided. Those along the Namib coast consist of a dark-coloured, briny clay which looks dry but in fact conceals a soggy substrate. I have seen a vehicle sunk nose-first into this mess, with the back wheels high up in the air.

Salt pans are also to be found in regions such as the Northern Cape, and especially in Botswana. My advice is to avoid driving on them, not only because of the obvious danger of getting stuck. If many vehicles, each making its own track, cross a pan, the resulting scars will spoil the natural beauty of these places. If you are forced to cross a salt pan, inspect it first on foot. if there is an existing track, stick to it. If it has recently rained, stay off the pan under all circumstances.

Beach driving has become very restricted in some places. In areas controlled by municipalities, where beaches are used for recreation, beach driving poses a danger to bathers and playing children and is prohibited by local ordinance or law. There are also prohibitions against beach driving dictated by the needs of conservation, for example the sensitive coastal dunes and sea turtle breeding grounds of northern KwaZulu-Natal. We should respect these regulations.

On average, though, driving on the hard intertidal strip results in virtually no damage to the environment, a fact that has been attested to by marine researchers in Namibia. Initially, it was thought that compacting of the sand by passing vehicles posed a threat to white mussels and other creatures. However, research has shown that the threat is negligible.

If you are forced to drive on the deep sand above the intertidal strip, the principles for deep sand driving oulined earlier come fully into play. My advice is to follow existing tracks or, if your group consists of a few vehicles, to stay in the tracks left by the leading vehicle.

The following distance between vehicles should be enough to allow for safe stopping. As discussed earlier (*see* page 61), tailgating in such a situation can have dire consequences, as the second and third vehicles become 'glued' to the track in deep, clammy sand and it is difficult to climb out of the track to avert a crash.

MOUNTAINS

There are some spectacular 4x4 mountain routes in Southern Africa, and the scenery and plantlife to be seen *en route* make them well worth tackling. The Sani Pass in Lesotho (Kaoko Scale rating 3) and Van Zyl's Pass in Namibia (Kaoko Scale rating 4) are two well-known (and notorious) routes. Along some 4x4 routes, farming communities even offer facilities where you can stay overnight, for example the magnificent Hex River Valley 4x4 route in the Western Cape. A few of the older, gravelled passes, such as the Montagu Pass and the Swartberg Pass, both in the Western Cape, should not present too many problems except if it has rained and the roads are slippery. Use 4x4 mode without hesitation.

Off-roading in the mountains requires that you apply the same techniques used for driving on rocky ground. When faced with very steep terrain and hairpin bends, drive slowly, never be impatient and remain calm in difficult sections. Do not hesitate to use the lowest gear and diff lock. If your vehicle starts pendulating sideways, stop and wait for the swaying to subside, then continue slowly forward. However, if it is becoming dangerous, off-load your luggage from the roof carrier.

Passengers should remain inside the vehicle as this serves to stabilise it, but, if the vehicle angles too much to one side during a bad stretch, get some of the passengers to hang on to the high side of the vehicle. Drive dead slowly and see that you do not crush anybody against the side of the mountain! Off-road vehicles are notorious for their wide turning circles, which can be quite unnerving when you have to negotiate hairpin bends. If you find yourself in such a situation, inch the vehicle forwards and backwards very slightly, as you may not have much space in which to manoeuvre. Remain calm and be patient – you will get around it.

A guardian angel

One day during the winter of 1995, I was descending Van Zyl's Pass, in Kaokoland, in my converted double-cab Land Cruiser. I was carrying the 'kitchen' for a large group of Swiss tourists, and was pulling a heavily laden trailer (with no brake).

I could feel that the vehicle was moving awkwardly, as if it was pulling me to the left, towards the precipice. Halfway down the pass, I stopped and, with the help of my assistants, inspected the vehicle. We found nothing wrong or even unusual.

So off we went, down the sandy flats of the Marienfluss. Eventually, with the camp site about a kilometre away, I suddenly felt that the vehicle was becoming sluggish and unable to pull. I changed into third gear to no avail, then shifted down to second. When I looked in my side rear-view mirror, I saw to my horror that the loading box had become totally loosened from its brackets and was hanging in the air like a tip-truck.

Apparently, what had occurred was that the chassis had broken just behind the wheel arches while we were in Van Zyl's Pass, and gave its swan song in the Marienfluss. I could just imagine what could have happened if it had snapped completely in the pass. To this day, I believe that guardian angels carried me down and allowed me to stop at a convenient place.

SNOW

Snow is not a common occurence throughout most of Southern Africa, the only exceptions being the Maluti Mountains of Lesotho and parts of the Drakensberg, KwaZulu-Natal. Off-road driving in snowy conditions requires the off-roader to make use of the same techniques as for driving on sand and mud (*see* pages 60 and 84).

As the road surface can be very slippery if snow has fallen, drive slowly in low range with the diff lock on, and deflate the tyres to the same pressure you would use for sand and mud driving. As is the case for mud, tyres with more aggressive (i.e., deeper) lugs are better suited for snow.

In snow, the vehicle will respond as it does in slippery mud, with the tail breaking away and the front wheels failing to respond to the direction of turning. If the vehicle starts to slide, turn the front wheels in the opposite direction to which the nose is moving; if they do not follow the turn, slow down immediately and stop, reverse two paces and then slowly accelerate. In very snowy conditions, it is advisable to have at least one set of snow chains around the back wheels. However, these are difficult to find on the Southern African market.

In sub-zero temperatures, special steps should be taken to ensure that the engine will start – especially diesel engines, as diesel fuel tends to become waxy in cold conditions. Gadgets are available from Europe for pre-heating the engine, but, if you do not have one of these, you could cover the bonnet with blankets and take turns to start the engine every hour to retain the heat, or you could drain the diesel into jerry cans and store these in a warmer place. Closely monitor your heat gauge and, if your engine remains cold, cover the front of the radiator with cardboard or anything that will lessen the flow of air. I have seen people removing the vehicle's

fan belt, but I do not advise doing this as you may unwittingly also remove the belt that drives the water pump (*see also* page 86). Fortunately, most 4x4s can handle extreme cold, provided that the thermostat is in good working order.

MUD, STREAMS AND RIVERS

It is important to cover these conditions together as they invariably occur together. Throughout most of Southern Africa, we are faced with fast-flowing rivers and streams that quickly become torrents during the rainy season. Mud invariably follows, and can be dangerous. My advice is as follows:

• When you are faced with a fast-flowing river or stream, and are in any doubt, simply stay put. You will have to wait for it to subside. On more than one occasion in the Namib, I have come up against raging rivers occasioned by rains falling far off in the hinterland. To judge whether it was right to cross, I would sink a stick into the mud at the water's edge to serve as a reference mark; after an hour, I could tell how fast the river was rising (or falling). If it was afternoon,

I prepared to camp until the next morning. If the river was receding quite quickly in the morning, I knew that I would be able to cross by the afternoon.

• Rivers always leave a quagmire. In certain cases, it is worth the effort to scout up- or downstream to find a place where the shore is made of rocks or flat stones and use this as a ford. If you cannot find a harder surface, you will have to wade into the mud and receding water to test the viscosity of the mud, as well as the strength and depth of the stream. With this knowledge, you can decide whether to cross.

Before you cross, ask yourself certain questions: Is my vehicle's air intake high enough so water won't be sucked in? Is the mud too viscous (or too deep)? Is my vehicle (and, perhaps, the trailer) heavy enough to withstand the force of the water? If the water is up to your waist and you have to struggle against the flow, then you must not ford the river; wait it out for another hour or so and then test it again.

• Once you have decided to make the crossing, see to it that your tyres

are deflated as you would for sand (*see* page 60) to give your vehicle more flotation and grip, select 4x4 mode – normally low or second gear (depending on the size and torque of your engine) – and do not attempt to change gears until you reach the other bank safely. If you change gears in deep mud, the momentary loss of power may be enough to bog you down.

When crossing a body of water that reaches halfway up your door sills, a wave builds up ahead of the vehicle as the mass of water is pushed away. This wave is a good sign, as it helps to keep the engine bay relatively dry. If it starts foaming or breaking over your bonnet, it is a sign that your speed is too high and you should slow down – it should be a smooth pressure wave in front of the vehicle.

It is vital to keep up a steady speed, so as not to allow the tyres to break the crust of the river bed and sink in. Do not apply too much fuel, as this could lead to the tyres spinning and bog you down.

• In places where there is a lot of standing or very slow-moving water, such as the Okavango in Botswana, other factors come into play. There may be crocodile and hippo in the area, and, if you wade barefoot into the river to test it, you could end up as lunch for a crocodile! In most bodies of standing water, sediments have settled and even become quite hard. However, if you can't wade in to test the water and mud, or if the water is so murky that you can't see the bottom, my advice is to stay away. In such cases, I've always followed existing tracks without a problem – and I've always found existing tracks. If there really are no tracks to follow, you will have to bite the bullet and test the water – after spending some time to see if there are crocodile or hippo about.

There are a few technical aspects to bear in mind before crossing mud, streams and rivers:

• If you have to travel through large bodies of standing water, it is worth investing in a snorkel, as well as watertight covers for the distributor and spark plugs (petrol vehicles only; diesels don't use spark plugs and have no distributor).

• There is no doubt that a broad radial tyre, preferably with very

aggressive lugs, and well deflated, works the best in water or mud.

• Finally, if you frequently have to cross rivers or bodies of standing water, it is a better idea to remove the vehicle's fan belt so as not to damage the fan. I wish to stress that this should only be done where removal will not interfere with other important engine functions (such as water pump circulation). Fording will cool the radiator and oil sump, but it is very important to put the fan belt back on as soon as you finish the crossing. Most fans nowadays have a viscous coupling, which means that, if the fan is immersed in water, the coupling will slip and even stop. If this is the case, it may not be necessary to remove the fan belt if you will only be making one or two crossings of smaller bodies of water.

DUST
The worst dust imaginable must be on the banks of river systems running through the Namib Desert. This dust is as fine as baby powder, and acts just like water once it gets into the engine, effectively causing your vehicle to stall.

If you have been driving in extremely dusty conditions, take out the air cleaner's element and gently tap it to remove the dust particles. This will help to clean the element. If you have an electric air pump, simply blow the air cleaner element from the inside. A word of advice: paper filter air cleaners are superior to oil-pan types in these conditions.

GETTING STUCK

You are bound to get stuck at some time or other, so be prepared for it. Vehicles tend to get stuck mostly in sand or mud, although there are exceptions. I will focus here on techniques to recover your vehicle from sand and mud.

• To make the tyre surface as broad as possible, deflate your tyres even further than you normally would. Many drivers are cautious about making the tyres nearly flat, but you can deflate them to 0.7–0.6 bar in front and 1.0–0.9 bar at the back without damaging them. They will also remain safely on the rim, so long as the wheels don't start spinning. As soon as you are out of trouble, inflate them again.

• Try to rock the vehicle gently backwards and forwards a few times by releasing and depressing the clutch slightly. This rocking motion sometimes compacts the surface enough to get the vehicle free.

• If you are an over-eager driver, then your vehicle could easily get bogged down to the chassis, or worse, to the floorboard. If this happens, the only course of action open to you is to use your high-lift jack to jack up the front and back of the vehicle, and to pack stones underneath the wheels. Make sure that the track between the front and back wheels is also packed with stones, sticks or whatever hard material you can find. Dig away all humps that may have developed in front of the wheels.

• It is essential that you include a broad, thick piece of timber as part of your vehicle's basic equipment. If you are stuck in mud or soft sand, the weight of the vehicle will merely press the jack into the ground once the vehicle is jacked up. The timber acts as a larger base for the jack, and serves to stabilise it.

• Sand plates are a wonderful aid if you are stuck (*see* page 46). Once I got stuck in a place where there was absolutely no vegetation or stones to pack under my wheels, and I decided from then on always to carry sand plates.

Use your shovel to clear away the 'dune' of excess sand in front of all tyres. Make a furrow, level with the area of the back tyres and in front of them, into which the sand plates will fit. Make sure the end of each sand plate fits tightly under-neath the tyre, start the engine, and gently – very gently – pull away so that there is no wheel spin. Once on the sand plates, the vehicle will soon pick up momentum.

When I'm in a hurry, I don't even bother with all the preparations: I simply slip the high-lift jack onto the back bumper, jack up the vehicle, slip the sand plates under the back tyres and Bob's your uncle.

• Finally, a word about winches: A winch can be an extremely useful

The sand anchor

Occasionally, I have got bogged down in the Namib without a tree or rock in sight to use as an anchor. In such desperate circumstances, one solution is make use of your spare wheel to fashion your own 'sand anchor' for the winch. First, attach your tow rope to the spare wheel. Then, bury the wheel as deep as possible in the sand; attach the winch cable to the shackle (if a shackle is used); put the jack base plate (the piece of timber described above) underneath the tow cable where it enters the ground at the burrowed tyre; and winch away. The timber will prevent the cable cutting a groove into the soft sand.

If you are badly stuck, it will be necessary for you and your party to lighten the vehicle. You will have to unpack your luggage before using the winch or tow ropes. If you are towing a trailer, it stands to reason that you should unhitch it before using the winch.

Take great care when using the winch. If the snatch block, tow rope or even the cable snaps, the rebound is deadly. Everyone in the group should stand away as far as possible during such an operation.

piece of equipment to have (*see page 43*). However, you could easily overtax the winch if your vehicle is completely bogged down. To prevent this from happening, ensure that you dig away all humps that have built up in front of the wheels, and use snatch blocks for extra torque.

THINGS THAT TEND TO BREAK

Certain vehicle parts are more prone than others to breakage or wear in off-road conditions. The following are the items that tend to leave you with a problem.

• *Shock absorbers*: Use only the shock absorbers prescribed for your vehicle, or heavy-duty, off-road shocks. Do not use those types which can be inflated.

• *Fuel tank*: Always carry a fuel tank repair stick in case you get a hole in the fuel tank. If you do not have a repair stick, try to block the hole with Sunlight soap.

• *Fuel line*: Tighten the clamps on the fuel line if there are leaks and carry 2 metres of extra fuel line pipe and spare clamps.

• *Radiator*: Your vehicle may start to overheat at some point, in which case you will need to inspect the radiator thoroughly. Sometimes you will clearly be able to see water spouting from a tiny hole, or you may find that the radiator fluid's residue is at the point of leaking. Let the radiator cool off and plug the leaks with Indian Cement or Bars' Leaks. The plugging material normally takes hold very quickly. Fill up the radiator before driving off, and check it again after you have driven for a while.

• *Fuel pump*: This very important part can leave you standing at awkward places. Take a spare fuel pump along or have one installed with the extra fuel tank so that you can easily switch fuel lines.

• *Fan belt*: Always carry two spares, as brand-new fan belts can break and damage the radiator fan. Make sure the spare belts fit!

• *Master and/or slave cylinders*: You will be in real trouble if these break, so have them serviced and all rubber seals replaced if those on your vehicle are over a year old.

Facing Fear

In off-roading, there always comes a time when one has to face fear. There have been times when I have had that copper taste in my mouth.

One of these occurred during the dry, hot season, when I had to go through the thick sands of the Kaudom Game Reserve north of Bushman-land. Many kilometres away, I could see smoke columns from several bush fires – a common enough sight in late winter. These fires are beneficial to a certain extent – Africa is a continent of droughts and fires – and huge flocks of birds of prey are attracted to the conflagrations as the flames drive their prey from their hiding places.

While stopped at a water hole called Leeupan, we became so immersed in our bird-watching that we did not notice that the wind direction had changed and that the fire was heading for us. I had five jerry cans of diesel tied down, but completely exposed, on the back of my trailer. When I realised that the fire was heading for us, I drove off immediately, minutes before the fire would have envelopped our road.

Then fate struck. Suddenly, my vehicle overheated – right in the path of the fire, which was travelling toward us with the terrifying sound of an approaching steam engine. The vehicle's radiator had sprung a leak. i got out and cooled the radiator by pouring water over it, whilst my assistant further deflated the tyres of both the vehicle and the trailer to give us better grip and flotation.

The fire darted over the road in front of us and behind us, but some-how seemed to hesitate in the middle. Suddenly, it appeared as though a tunnel had miraculously opened up in front of us through the flames and smoke. I started up the Land Cruiser and drove it through the opening. We got out safely, but were quite shaken. Yet another instance of my guardian angels at work!

• *Engine mountings*: Ensure that you have a mechanic check these before setting off on your trip.

• *Hybrid vehicles*: An example of this is a Land Rover with a Ford V6 engine. Stay clear of hybrid vehicles, as they can develop gearbox or clutch troubles if not put together by a professional engineering firm. I have seen Toyota double-cabs fitted with 3,5-litre Rover engines which overheated constantly.

MAKING A PLAN

It is remarkable how individual ingenuity comes into play when one is faced with mechanical breakdowns and difficulties. Consider the following examples:

• A friend of mine was stranded with two flat tyres, but without a tube repair kit. He limped home by filling the tyres with sand.

• Another person survived a leaking radiator by stuffing it with biscuits. It worked, and got him home.

• The cover of my petrol pump was knocked off by a stone. The holder for my anti-perspirant was the same size. It leaked, but I got home.

7

WHAT TO TAKE

It is always a problem to decide what to pack when going on a trip. Care must be taken in this matter, as you must guard against packing too much – thereby adding to the overall weight of the vehicle. The following are the minimum that you will need for a comfortable camping experience.

TENT

The dome (igloo) tent is superior to any other type of tent. It is quick and easy to pitch and take down, and is usually insect- and rain-proof. There is a wide variety to choose from, ranging from lightweight, nylon tents to more durable, but heavier, tents made from canvas. I strongly recommend that you buy a canvas tent, as it offers greater resistance to fire, ultraviolet light and water, and provides better protection against wild animals than a nylon tent.

These days, it has also become popular to buy roof tents. These are easy to erect and store, do not take up space inside the vehicle and offer protection against wild animals and insects (*see* page 49). However, if you need to use your vehicle, you will have to take down the tent before driving off!

When choosing a tent, base your decision on the following requirements: you must be able to stand upright in it; it must have a solid PVC floor (not a woven one) with a mud wall (an upward extension of the floor on all sides to keep flowing water out) of at least 30 centimetres in height on each side; it should have mosquito nets over the doors and windows; and a fly sheet over the top in case of bad weather.

CARING FOR YOUR TENT

Here are a few suggestions for taking care of your tent:

• Before erecting the tent, always make sure that there are no thorns, sharp sticks or stones on the ground which could damage the floor.

• Since people usually put pressure on their front foot to balance themselves as they step inside a tent, use the tent bag as a mat/carpet at the entrance to the tent. By doing this, you will reduce wear and tear on the floor.

• Do not rest sharp-edged objects on the floor of the tent. Glue some pieces of old carpeting to the base of your stretcher so that it exerts less pressure on the floor.

• To help keep out the dust and sand, place a canvas or plastic mat (you could also use your bakkie's PVC blocks) outside the entrance to the tent.

• *Never* use candles, paraffin or gas lamps inside the tent. Nylon tents, in particular, will ignite with astonishing speed (*see* pages 110 and 118).

• Vacuum the walls of the tent after a trip to remove dust and grime.

• Before storing the tent, rub down the metal tent struts with a cloth dampened in paraffin. This will prevent rusting. Store your tent in a dry place.

• In the past, canvas would rot if it was packed away while still damp. Today, the canvas contains an acrylic fibre that offers more resistance to rot. Nevertheless, avoid storing your tent if it is damp, as this may cause it to smell.

PROTECTING THE TENT
Since ultraviolet light causes the most damage to tents in Africa, you will need to impregnate your tent at least once a year with a canvas impregnation compound to keep it in a good condition. To do this, I suggest that you adhere to the following procedure:

• Erect the tent and scrub down the walls, both inside and outside, with a medium-strength solution of laundry soap (washing powder) and water. Hose the tent down to wash off all the soap, and allow it to dry.

• Mix the canvas impregnation compound with turpentine at

a ratio of 1:9 (1 turpentine to 9 compound) and stir it thoroughly. The compound contains a wax which makes the tent waterproof and protects against ultraviolet light.

• Apply the mixture to the outside of the tent with a paint brush or spray gun, giving special attention to the seams. Allow to dry, and leave the tent to stand for two or three days until the strong smell of turpentine has subsided. Using a spray gun gives a professional look to the application.

• After the tent has dried, spray the tent with Peripel insect repellent to keep the mosquitoes away. This treatment will last until the next time you wash the tent.

• Rub candle wax onto all the zipper surfaces. Do this more than once a year as it helps to preserve the zips and eases functioning.

STORING A DOME TENT

Before storing a dome tent, fold it up as follows (*see* illustrations):

• Leave the frame standing and unhook the tent.

• Pull the top of the tent either to the left or right, away from the door so that it lies down square on the ground. Take over the other side in the same way.

1. Unhook the tent from the frame.

2. Pull the tent to the left or the right.

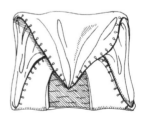

3. Fold one side over.

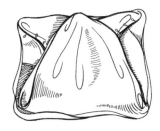

4. Fold the next side over.

5. Fold over again and roll up the tent.

• Pull the tent open (it should fold open) to cover the door and then back, exposing the door. The tent is now and ready to roll up.

• Finally, take down the frame, fold it to fit into the tent bag – the struts fit into each other, but are held together by a chain or PVC rope – and store the tent in a dry place.

FURNITURE

• *Beds*: Stretchers are the most durable and versatile of sleeping equipment. Air mattresses are quite popular these days, but these can easily deflate if pricked by a thorn or sharp stone. Another option is to sleep on a hiking mat, but you would not be very comfortable during winter in the Kalahari.

Fold a blanket double and place it on top of the stretcher. It is quite important to do this during winter as the blanket will help to protect you against the cold ground. Roll out your sleeping bag on top of the blanket. Eiderdown sleeping bags are very warm and cosy, but the ultimate is the sleeping roll with built-in mattress, sheets, blankets and pillow. Although a sleeping roll is bulky and takes up space, I could not travel without one.

• *Chairs*: There is a wide variety of camping chairs available these days, but I still find the good old deck chair very comfortable. If you have been sitting in the car the whole day, *riempiestoele* are not really what you want to sit on.

• *Table*: It is advisable to buy a sturdy, folding table made out of sheet metal. Wooden tables have slats that can break, and plastic and

The cold Kalahari

Most of my formative years were spent in the Namib Desert. When I first entered the Kalahari Desert, in Bushmanland, I was unprepared for the bitterly cold winter nights. Due to its proximity to the Atlantic Ocean, the Namib never gets very cold, and so I was accustomed to sleeping on the ground with only a few blankets to cover me. Naturally, I did the same when I first travelled to Bushmanland.

I very quickly learned that the opposite was true in the Kalahari. Apparently, the sand of the Kalahari consists of a very high proportion of silica, which has virtually no heat-retention properties. The minute the sun dips below the horizon, the hot sand starts to cool rapidly. By nightfall, it is very cold indeed.

From that time onward, I saw to it that my sleeping roll, with its built-in mattress, was laid out before sunset, while the sand was still hot. Thus, my bed at least retained some of the heat of the sand. As I grew older – and perhaps softer and wiser – I started using a stretcher covered in a double-folded blanket, and laid my sleeping roll on top of that.

aluminium folding tables will fall to pieces after a while. Sheet-metal tables are available in different sizes to suit your family's needs, but they do tend to be too high when you are sitting on a chair. To rectify this, simply use a hacksaw to shorten the table's legs.

• Another handy idea is to take along some trays. Using them will allow you to have meals around the fire instead of seated at the table. This can be quite sociable.

COOKING UTENSILS

• *The potjie*: This is a very useful item, although it will become rusty with time and is difficult to pack. I suggest that you have a sturdy wooden box made, into which the potjie will fit tightly. To prevent the potjie from rusting, always clean it immediately after use and, once it is dry, oil the inside slightly with cooking oil while the pot is still hot.

• *The ladle*: Invest in a solid ladle that won't rust. Those with plastic handles that are fixed to the bowl with studs are really useless.

• **The grill**: You must have a grill with sides that fold over so that your meat doesn't fall into the sand when you turn it over.

• **'Skottelbraai'**: It is very useful to take one of these along for frying bacon, sausages, eggs and even vegetables.

• The apparatus on which you rest your potjie or braai grill is important – bear in mind that you may not always be able to find stones to use for this purpose. The sketches shown on this page could serve as a guide for the DIY enthusiast.

• **Pots and kettle**: Cheap aluminium ones will serve you well. To keep them clean and shiny without having to scrub them, mix a little water with some washing powder and whip it into a thick paste. Cover the outside of the pots or kettle with this paste. The soap will turn black from the fire but, after a quick rinse, these items will be completely clean. You can cook up to three times in this way before rinsing them.

• **Crockery**: Although cheap plastic crockery becomes scratched and worn, it is functional and doesn't break. Melamine utensils are quite durable except that the cups tend to crack if you pour hot liquid into them on a cold winter morning. I prefer to use china, as it is more attractive and can be thoroughly cleaned. To prevent crockery from breaking, I stack the plates in a metal ammunition box with rubber sponge glued to the inside and thin

A mesh grill with folding metal legs is ideal for placing your potjie over a fire.

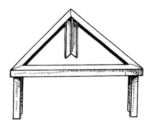

This handy metal triangle, on which the potjie sits, also incorporates folding legs.

sponge placed between every plate. This works very well for me.

STORAGE BOXES

Whether they are made from sheet metal, plastic or aluminium, the many different types of boxes that are available are all sturdy, long-lasting and functional.

• *Plastic boxes*: For the past five years, I have stored my goods in two different types of plastic boxes. Although I have travelled over some of the worst roads in Africa, they have given me no problems.

The first type is a large box with a lid. The box tapers down slightly to the bottom. The other box I use is the so-called ammunition kist (chest), which is smaller but easier to store. These kists are available in different colours, which helps you to remember what items are stored in which box. Although plastic boxes do fray around the edges, they can last you a lifetime if they are not exposed to too much ultraviolet light (which leads to cracking).

• *Sheet-metal kists*: These are strong, durable and amazingly light. The advantage of these boxes is that the

lids are hinged, enabling you to lock up your goods when necessary.

• *Aluminium kists*: These boxes are also strong, durable and light, but are much more expensive.

COOLER BOXES

There are some lovely cooler boxes on the market today. These are generally made from durable plastic, some with sheet metal or aluminium sheet on the outside. Although they are long-lasting, their insulation is only about 3 centimetres thick – too thin to be really effective. I prefer to use a handmade cooler box constructed out of galvanised sheet metal, with 6-centimetre-thick insulation walls. The disadvantage of this type of cooler box is that it should only be opened once a day (for not longer than a minute), should not be exposed to direct sunlight for more than five minutes and should always be completely covered with blankets.

• Bars of solid ice will stay frozen in the cooler box for much longer than ice cubes – ice cubes do not last even half as long as the bars. Freezer bags, otherwise known as ice bricks, are quite effective if you use enough of them. They contain a liquid which thaws very slowly, and freezer bags remain relatively dry in comparison to the ice bars. However, you will need to have a freezer to re-freeze the bags (or bricks) once they have defrosted. Remember to drain the melted water from your cooler box after the third day as water causes the ice to thaw more quickly.

• Pack your cooler box sensibly. Place the food that you will be eating towards the end of the tour on the bottom, and put the items that you will need for your first few meals on the top. This type of arrangement means you won't have to rummage around too much and your cooler box won't have to stand open while you look for something.

• When you are packing fruit and vegetables into your cooler box prior to leaving, I suggest you first cool them in the fridge with a few freezer bricks, then put them into the cooler box. When you are on tour in winter, keep the box open at night to allow the excess water vapour to evaporate, as otherwise it can cause the fruit and vegetables to rot. The contents will remain cool. In the morning, before sunrise, close the lid and cover the box with a blanket for extra insulation.

THE FRIDGE/FREEZER

After a long, hot, dusty drive, it is wonderful to be able to grab an ice-cold drink from the fridge. Outdoor and camping magazines are filled with advertisements for mobile fridge/freezers, and the choice can be quite confusing. Manufacturers offer the public little advice to help them make the right choice, so before you buy one of these units it is important to know the advantages and disadvantages of the different types.

There are basically two types of fridge/freezer on the market: those driven by a pump and those driven by convection. The latter, also called a caravanning fridge/freezer, works on the principle of an electrical, gas or paraffin element, while the pump-driven type operates in the same way as an ordinary household fridge. The pump-driven fridge/freezer is far superior to the convection-driven type.

In order to function efficiently, convection fridges need to be completely level (some manufacturers even build in a spirit level). However, the tough conditions you will encounter in off-roading make this virtually impossible to achieve. There is also the added danger of gas exploding or petrol igniting.

Although pump-driven fridges are much more expensive, the pumps have been specially built to withstand the wear and tear of off-roading. A pump-driven fridge will keep your food frozen for as long as the vehicle's battery lasts, and so represents a very sound long-term investment. The fridge is switched off at night to save the battery; as long as the fridge is not opened, your food will remain cold until the next morning when you switch on again.

THE SHOWER OR BATH

It is important (and pleasant) to keep clean, even when you or your group are many miles from civilisation. I remember how a friend dutifully lugged a large, old-fashioned, galvanised tub on top of his vehicle because his wife would not go camping unless she

could have a hot bath every evening. You could go to the other extreme and simply fill an old bucket with water to wash yourself. I have some better ideas:

• There are several types of showers available that hold water in a black PVC bag; attached to the bag is a hose, valve and small shower head. If you leave this type of shower lying in the sun for a while, the solar-heated water will give you a lovely hot shower. However, the bag doesn't hold very much water; once the hot water has been used up, or if someone else wants to have a shower, you'll have to leave it in the sun again to heat up more water. You could always fill the bag with warm water from the fire, but the idea is make use of solar energy. The bag is also not very sturdy.

• Another idea is the old army-type 2-gallon PVC shower that is hoisted up a tree. It is better than the black bag described above, as you can quickly top it up with hot water from the fire, and it holds enough water so that four people can have showers. However, this type of shower is bulky and very heavy when filled. In addition, if there are no trees in the area – and this is a strong possibility – you will not be able to have a shower.

• *Privacy*: To shower, you will also need some privacy. Both types of shower need to be hoisted up, and this requires the construction of some kind of screen or area to ensure privacy for the person using the shower. Screens can be erected without too much trouble, but this takes time; when you reach a camping spot after a full day's drive, it becomes quite a job to set up tents, kitchen, toilet and beds, and then still have to put up a shower screen. One of the best arrangements that I have seen is constructed as follows:

• For the enclosure, fix two pieces of pipe on top of the vehicle's roof under the roof carrier. Slide a 1.5-metre U-shaped rod into the ends of these pipes so that it fits in snugly while you are driving. When you need to shower, pull out the rod until it protrudes a metre or so from the side of the vehicle (*see* illustration above). Hang a thin plastic curtain from the U-shaped

rod. For a finishing touch, you could place PVC liners or blocks on the ground to stand on.

• To make the shower, buy a plastic bucket and a Gardena-type snap-on hose valve. Drill a neat hole through the bottom of the bucket, to which you firmly attach the hose valve. Make sure to buy a hose valve that will block the flow of water if the hose becomes disconnected – for

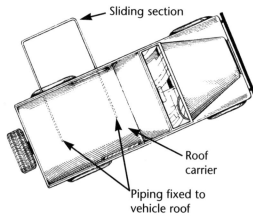

Sliding section

Roof carrier

Piping fixed to vehicle roof

Attach a shower rail to the vehicle roof.

instance, if you need to fill the bucket up quickly. Attach a garden hose with a male plug for the bucket valve on one end and for the other end a plastic telephone-type shower head.

To regulate the flow of water, cut the hose somewhere in the middle and insert a Gardena-type hose regulator. Place the plastic bucket (with the shower line attached) on the roof carrier and fill a galvanised bucket with water and heat it up on the fire. Then, simply pour the warm water into the plastic bucket, open the valve and step under the stream of water. Each bucket will shower at least two people (*see* illustration below).

• To me, the ultimate shower is that operated by a permanently installed pump, which runs off the vehicle's battery on 12 volts. This pump can be fitted at a convenient spot inside your vehicle. The pump has an inlet as well as an outlet pipe, over which you can push tight-fitting rubber hoses. Place the free end of the inlet hose in a bucket of warm water; the free end of the outlet hose is fitted with a hand-held telephone-type shower head. As soon as you switch on the pump, you will get a lovely shower. The pump-driven shower is very convenient, as you do not have to lug buckets of water onto the roof carrier.

THE TOILET

If you do not enjoy going into the bush with a spade, you will have no choice but to take along some type of toilet. There are two options:

• *The 'porta potty' mobile toilet with flushing facilities*: This will serve your purpose very well, but it is a bit bulky. However, if you do decide to take one along, ensure that you use an environment-friendly additive (added to the water when flushing.

• *A fold-up chair-type 'loo'*: Simple to make, this type of loo is in effect a simple chair with a toilet seat.

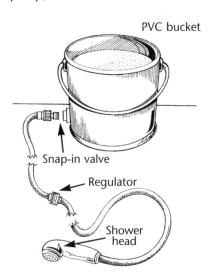

PVC bucket

Snap-in valve

Regulator

Shower head

A bucket and hose make a fine shower.

To make one yourself – assuming you are a DIY person – take two U-shaped pieces of light, square metal tubing. The tubes can be fitted into the pegs of the square frame that holds the toilet seat. The legs can be taken off to make it easier to store. I have found that this type of model works very well. Of course, using it requires that you first dig a hole in the ground, over which the 'chair' is placed.

YOUR RUBBISH

With all the items that you need on a trip, it is easy to overlook the fact that you will also produce a lot of refuse. Because of this 'gap' in their planning, many people find they have to fit a growing amount of refuse into their vehicle or trailer.

• The best solution to the refuse problem is to make sure that you have a supply of sturdy refuse bags, with enough space in the vehicle to carry your refuse until you reach a municipal dump. The normal black/green/yellow kitchen refuse bags are simply not strong enough, though. You should carry strong raffia-type bags into which your normal kitchen bag can be fitted.

• Compress tins, boxes and other refuse as much as possible, and see to it that the bag is securely closed when you drive off. Normally, the outside of a trailer is the best place to carry such a bag, as long as it is well tied down.

• *Never* bury your refuse. It will quickly be dug up by scavengers and spoil the environment.

CLOTHING

The savanna regions of the Southern African interior are known for their hot summers (with short, heavy rainfalls) and cold winter nights, but mild to hot winter days. The wide variation in temperatures that you are likely to encounter sometimes requires a change of clothing in the course of the day.

• Be sure to pack T-shirts, jeans, shorts, socks, shoes (or boots) and sandals/strops. Always take a very warm jacket along, even in summer, as nights can be surprisingly cold after it has rained.

• Never wear bright colours, as they distract wildlife. Note that tsetse flies are attracted to the colours blue, black and white (*see* page 121). The most appropriate and practical colours for the bush are khaki, olive-green and grey.

• When walking through typical grass savanna, wear high-ankle boots and puttees or gaiters. Boots with canvas uppers are generally not recommended as grass seeds can penetrate them.

• An army-type rain poncho is extremely handy during the rainy season, except when hiking in the mountains, where more appropriate clothing should be worn.

• I recommend adding a solution of Peripel insect repellent to your laundry rinse water, as this will cause your clothes to give off a poisonous substance which will kill mosquitoes when they land. The solution is effective for up to four washes and does not have any harmful effects on humans.

• In malarial areas, always wear trousers, thick socks, high-ankle boots and long-sleeved shirts in the evenings. Research in the Kruger National Park has shown that mosquitoes mostly attack the area between the knee and the ankle.

• A cap or hat is a necessity.

LAUNDRY

To keep your clothes clean, you can construct a simple but effective 'washing machine'. This contraption takes advantage of the movement of your vehicle or trailer to clean your clothes. Buy a 20- to 25-litre plastic drum with a lid held in place by a clamp around the edge. Tie this drum to your vehicle or trailer, put in your laundry, add hot water and soap, close the lid and drive off. During the day, the movement of the vehicle will shake the laundry around gently, and, when you reach your destination in the evening, your laundry will be clean. You can then rinse and hang it out to dry. Use a bio-friendly detergent.

• If the fancy takes you, it is possible to iron your clothes by heating up a solid iron on the gas primus, or by using an old-fashioned iron into which you can put the embers from the fire. Gas-operated irons are also available.

8

THE CAMP SITE

CHOOSING A CAMP SITE

Always look for a camp site at least one and a half hours before darkness sets in. There are few things more chaotic, unpleasant and dangerous than setting up camp in the dark.

• Never camp near lakes, rivers, dams or water holes. This is especially true in the arid areas of Southern Africa, as predators, pachyderms and poisonous insects tend to congregate near water during the night. Not only will you disturb these animals, who sometimes travel long distances to find water, but you may set up camp on an elephant footpath, which could be very dangerous.

In the dunes of north-eastern Namibia, Botswana and some parts of Zimbabwe, the 'streets' between the dunes are clay-based, so that water more readily forms small dams or pans. This is the favourite haunt of the baboon spider (*bobbejaanspinnekop*) and the scorpion.

Hippo leave the rivers at night to forage; it is well documented that they are disturbed by camp fires and that they have on occasion tried to stomp them out. Many people are unaware that hippo are the biggest killers of human beings in Africa. The Himba people of the Kaokoveld in Namibia have reported that crocodile sometimes leave the river and stalk their goats. I have seen a dog with a large laceration on its face after an attack by a crocodile – an attack that took place at least 45 metres from the Kunene River course.

My advice, therefore, is to camp at least three kilometres away from rivers, streams or drinking holes. If you find yourself near a river, look for a safe place, preferably at the top of a high bank.

Inspect your chosen camp site carefully, and watch out for the following telltale signs:

• *An elephant footpath*: This is a clearly visible, metre-wide footpath in the bush, covered with a carpet of dung. The dung, incidentally, is one reason why these animals can enter your camp silently and undetected.

• *A hippo footpath*: Narrower than that of the elephant, a hippo footpath leads to a grazing area. The path itself, as well as the adjacent bushes, is often sprayed with dung.

• *Scorpion nests*: Nesting sites or what seems like large concentrations of scorpions are found in certain areas of the Kalahari. Their holes are quite distinct from the round holes made by insects: a scorpion's hole is normally flat and shaped like a half-moon – to allow sufficient room for its pincers when it reverses into the hole. Scorpions generally shun full moon or bright, moonlit nights, as the small amount of ultraviolet light reflected by the moon lights up their bodies and makes them vulnerable to predators. They favour nights when there is sufficient cloud cover or no moon.

There are a number of other precautions to take:

• Gathering firewood in the dark is dangerous and difficult, and there is the possibility of picking up tamboti wood (*Spirostachys africana*). If you use this wood for braaiing when it is not completely dry, the whole group could fall ill: when green or insufficiently dry tamboti wood is burned, it gives off a poisonous gas; if this contaminates your meat, it could make you quite sick. Very old, dry wood doesn't pose such a problem, but even termites shun it. So, before gathering firewood from under a tree, test to see if it is tamboti by breaking off a leaf at the base of the tree. If the leaf exudes a white latex, do not use it.

• If you are camping in predator country, particularly where there are lion and hyaena, you must take precautions. Park the vehicles in a semi-circle, bumper to bumper, to form a 'laager'. Close the circle by erecting a barrier out of tarpaulins, and pitch the tents inside this barrier. Large animals, such as lion, hyaena and elephant, cannot distinguish depth, and perceive the surfaces of tents and tarpaulins as solid barriers. The tarpaulin should be wide and high enough to discourage these animals from jumping over; cheap, lightweight sheets of sackcloth can also be used. I strongly recommend that you follow the laager principle in Botswana and at places like Mana Pools in Zimbabwe.

• Do not set up camp in canyons or dry riverbeds during the rainy season, or even if there is the possibility of rain many kilometres from your camp site. Flash floods are a real danger to lives, and equipment and vehicles could be swept away. I have observed, on more than one occasion, how a dry riverbed can become a raging torrent in a matter of minutes.

• In some places, it is important to pay attention to the prevailing winds. The wind can be ferocious at the coast, and even across large bodies of water, like Lake Kariba in Zimbabwe. In the Namib Desert, a south-westerly wind blows almost

every evening, and only subsides around 9:00 pm. When setting up camp, you should park your vehicles so that they form the first line of protection against the wind, followed by the tents, then the tables and chairs and other equipment (*see* illustration on page 109). Build your fire downwind, at a safe distance from the vehicles and equipment. Obviously, the tent entrances must face the fire downwind. It is also handy to have shade nets permanently mounted on poles and anchored into the ground with a special peg, which has a ring into which the poles of the shade net fit. These nets effectively break the speed of the wind, making your stay at the camp site more pleasant.

THE CAMP FIRE

The camp fire is an integral part of camping in the African bush. What could be more enjoyable than spending an evening next to a crackling fire, reminiscing about the day's events, looking up at the stars and listening to the sounds of the owls? Although primus stoves and various other cooking appliances serve their purpose well,

A connoisseur elephant

In the late winter of 1997, I was camping at Mana Pools in Zimbabwe, where the resident bull elephant have the habit of visiting the camp each day towards dusk to forage on the seed pods that fall off the trees. This can be quite an unnerving experience, as they stand right next to your tent while they rock the trees with their foreheads to make more pods fall. Obviously, they are more used to the tourists than the tourists are to them.

On this evening, I met a group of three young wine farmers from the Western Cape who had set up their camp next to us. They had a small trailer still attached to their bakkie. A few paces away, they had opened a fine bottle of Pinotage, which was standing on a small wooden table with some wine glasses.

As an elephant approached our camp site, I told the farmers to sit quietly in their tent and wait out the animal's visit. The pachyderm, whose antics I observed keenly, climbed daintily over the trailer boom – without so much as touching the vehicle – and ever so daintily sniffed the bottle of wine.

He must have approved, because he turned on a 'tickey' (full circle) in the small space between the table and trailer and continued on around my tent – without spilling a drop of wine.

The young people were so relieved that they promptly offered me another bottle of Pinotage, which I accepted graciously and drank with the necessary respect. After all, if an elephant can behave like a connoisseur, then so can I!

they are really no substitute for the atmosphere provided by an open fire. Here are a few ideas on how to make a really good fire:

• Always try to build the fire within a circle of stones. This prevents the embers from rolling out, and contains the ash and dead coals.

• Break the firewood into pieces short enough to fit into the stone circle. Long branches sticking out can be dangerous obstructions.

• Some types of wood make better fires than others. The best wood is leadwood (*Combretum imberbe*). If this is not available, use camel thorn (*Acacia erioloba*) or old mopane wood (*Colophspermum mopane*)

• If you don't have fire lighters, first build the fire with dry grass and then add a liberal amount of dry twigs. Include a few thicker twigs to help to sustain the fire. Light the grass; as soon as the fire has taken well, slowly add firewood, but be careful not to smother the flames.

• To avoid veld fires, allow a safe distance between the fire and the vehicles, tents, gas or fuel. Never make a fire against a tree.

Wind direction

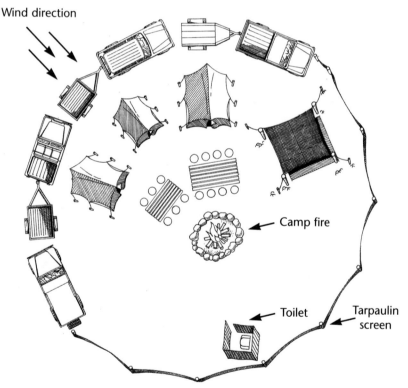

Camp fire

Toilet

Tarpaulin screen

Arrange your camp site to provide shelter from prevailing winds and predators.

Beautiful smoke

The smoke from a fire sometimes seems to follow you wherever you shift your chair. As a consolation, remember the old African saying: 'The smoke of a fire always follows a beautiful person'.

• Always be careful when gathering firewood (*see* page 106).

LIGHTING

Adequate lighting is vital. Weak or bad lighting can be dangerous, as accidents happen more easily when you can't see properly. Poor lighting also makes it frustrating to rummage in boxes for a particular item.

Due to their ultraviolet spectrum, very bright lights will attract a multitude of insects. At certain times of the year, especially after the rainy season, your camp site can become a very unpleasant place indeed if it is invaded by hordes of crawling and flying insects. On occasion, I have even seen a 100-candlepower gas light extinguished by hundreds of flying termites.

Baboon spiders (*bobbejaan-spinnekop*) may be large, hairy and fast, and look ominous, but they are, fortunately, quite harmless. If they are attracted by the lights of your camp, extinguish the lights for

a few minutes. The spiders will usually head off in another direction. However, if you have a really bad case of arachnophobia, the best thing you can do is take something for a headache and spend the night on your vehicle's roof.

The following is a list of lights that I can recommend, and some tips on how to use them correctly:

• The primus-type lantern which uses paraffin gives off a good light, but is very hot and should never be used inside a tent. The injector nozzles are prone to blockages, and unfortunately these lanterns are not supplied with yellow glass to ward off insects.

• Gas lamps screwed onto gas bottles (10-kilogram or more), are versatile, and can be fitted with various gadgets to ensure good lighting. They are available with different candlepower wicks, as well as yellow glass. You should keep a supply of wicks and nozzles on hand, as they have a tendency to get blocked.

• Smaller gas lights, specifically those with gas cartridges and a pizzo-type lighter, are amazing little lamps. Unfortunately, these do not have yellow glass.

• Tube lights, operated from your vehicle's cigarette lighter or battery terminal, are very effective and present no fire hazard. They are not available with a yellow covering; this can be rectified by sticking on yellow overlay plastic sheets. These come glued and ready for use.

• There are several lantern-type torches. Some can be charged from your vehicle's cigarette lighter, while others have their own solar panel or work with batteries. These torches are great in tents, as they can be suspended from the roof and are safe and cost-effective.

• There are several types of torches. A good, but costly, investment is the aluminium-bodied type available in gun and outdoor shops. However, I would not advise investing in a rechargeable torch, as the batteries don't seem to last.

• The so-called 'miner's headlamp' operates from small batteries and frees your hands – making it very useful in the kitchen.

• The common old paraffin lantern works very well; once filled up, it will burn through the night, although it does not generate a strong light. Leave at least one hanging all night in the camp, or even at the loo. If you add citronella oil to the paraffin (50 millilitres per litre), it will keep away insects, including mosquitoes.

• Candles are inadequate in the bush. Even those with mosquito-repellent properties are not effective.

9

THE KITCHEN

A well-organised kitchen will increase the enjoyment of your tour tremendously. Veld cooking, or cooking in the bush, is both a pleasure and a challenge, and practice makes perfect!

First-timers are sometimes quite nervous about cooking in the bush and tend to buy far too many pre-cooked meals to compensate for the lack of a real kitchen. Here are a few tips to help you along:

• Plan a menu for each day and keep to it. When planning your meals, study your itinerary carefully and work out the menu accordingly. For example, on some mornings you may want to depart early, in which case a brunch at 11:00 a.m. will be more suitable than a breakfast at 6:00 a.m. At other times, you may be in one place for a few days, which will give you time to prepare more elaborate meals.

• Use your menu to determine the amount of food that you will need, and buy groceries well in advance. I recommend doing this to avoid a final, frenzied rush before you depart on the trip, and to give you time to ensure that you have stocked up on everything you need. However, perishable items (such as vegetables, meat, eggs, etc.) should be bought only a day or two before leaving, to ensure freshness.

• Try to pack similar types of food together: keep tins in one box and items such as cereal, rice, mealie meal and pasta in another. Before packing tins into boxes, write the abbreviated name of the contents on top of the tin. This will save you a lot of hassle when searching for food, especially if it is getting dark.

• Disinfect your fruit and vegetables by washing them in a solution of

water and Milton steriliser fluid.
Certain vegetables, such as lettuce,
cannot be disinfected in this solution as they will turn brown.

• After thoroughly drying your
perishables, wrap them individually
in newspaper before packing them
into the fridge or cooler box. This
inhibits bacterial growth and keeps
the contents dry. Some perishable
items will last without any special
wrapping, particularly pumpkins,
gem squashes, potatoes, onions,
lemons and oranges. Inspect your
vegetables regularly, and get rid of
those which have gone bad.

• Fragile items, such as tomatoes,
should also be packed individually,
and separately from other items,
in a small carton in the fridge or
cooler box. This may be a tedious
job, but it is definitely safer. Eggs
are particularly vulnerable to
breakage; to keep them safe,
buy special plastic egg containers
for camping. Make sure that you
store eggs in a cool, dry place like
the fridge or cooler box. When
you want to use an egg, break it
into a saucer first and smell whether
it is still fresh.

• Avoid taking white meats (i.e. fish
pork, chicken and even veal) with
you on your trip, as they are highly
susceptible to salmonella infection.
All meat should be vacuum-packed
and deep-frozen before being stored
in the cooler box.

• As with your potjie, it is sensible
to pack your pots and pans in a
special container to prevent them
from rattling while you are on the
road. Choose pans with simple iron
handles; plastic handles will melt
when used over the open fire.
Pack the cutlery in a box, and keep
this separate from the other utensils
so you can find it quickly.

• Keep a box in your kitchen area
for storing detergent, scourers,
sponges, bleach, dishcloths, fire
lighters, braai tongs and even a
plastic drying rack for your dishes.
Take two plastic basins along to
use as a scullery. Nowadays, you
can purchase a fold-up scullery
stand, which can be a real asset
on any trip. The ultimate, of course,
is the complete fold-up kitchen
with room for a basin, gas stove
and other features. However, this
product is expensive.

Catering for nature

In my travels, I have had all kinds of problems with my kitchen. Once, elephant blocked my kitchen vehicle in the Huanib River Valley. On occasion, rain has delayed supper until breakfast, and, in Bushmanland, a dozen huge baboon spiders were attracted to my kitchen light.

Such difficulties are only to be expected. There are, however, both bigger and smaller pests to contend with. Some of these encounters I recall with amusement, though they certainly didn't seem funny at the time! For example, at Aba-Huab, Twyfelfontein, a hornbill and his family just loved to raid the goodies that I put out for breakfast or lunch.

At Ongongo Pool, in Namibia, a resident gerbil discovered that visitors carry delightful things to eat. When caught, he would sit there with his pleading brown eyes until he was gently removed. One night, he even gnawed the plastic off the frame of my glasses. When I go to Ongongo nowadays, I take precautions against 'Mickey' – as he has been christened – and leave some food for him, but far away from my kitchen.

The worst thieves must be the baboons at Serondella, in the Chobe National Park, Botswana, who would raid food boxes or tables with seeming impunity. One morning, one of them stole my last tin of jam – fortunately unopened – from the breakfast table. The curses uttered by my assistants and me were, fortunately, not understood by the group of Spanish doctors who were on safari with me.

I completely lost my temper and my dignity, and the struggle that ensued was something like a very bad rugby match. The baboon ducked through the bushes with the tin held tightly under his arm like a rugby back-liner. I followed hot on his heels, shouting and slinging stones. Eventually, I won and retrieved my tin of jam, to the great delight of my Spanish guests, who called out 'Eez nice show you give at breakfast, Jan'.

• When I go on a 4x4 trip, I insist on organising the kitchen area before I attend to the tents or anything else. Gather the firewood, collect the water and set up the table and lamp – it is important to do these chores first, as it takes time to prepare food. If you spend time sorting out the tents and other equipment before setting up your kitchen, your supper will not be ready for a very long time.

• It is of utmost importance that the kitchen area is well lit. If the cook wears a miner's headlamp (*see* page 111), this will leave his or her hands free and speed up preparations considerably.

• Try to have a good breakfast, a light lunch and a hearty supper. When staying over for a day in one place, use the extra time to prepare lunch for the following day. Cook rice or pasta to make different kinds of salads, or even put a special pudding in the fridge.

• I suggest that you draw up a list of chores for the group (*see* page 128). A proper division of labour ensures a well-organised and enjoyable trip.

A FEW RECIPES

I enter this field with a certain amount of trepidation, as I have seen men and women preparing food around a fire with all the zest and skill of a cordon bleu chef. Whatever you like to eat, there are a multitude of books on the market today containing recipes designed for use on camping and hiking trips.

When it comes to cooking, my bible is *Kook en Geniet* (*Cook and Enjoy*) by Mrs. S.J.A. de Villiers. First published in 1951, this is a standard book in Southern Africa; my own tattered copy dates from 1973 – the 30th edition! It tells you everything you need to know, and I've found that many overseas visitors, especially the French, love the recipes from it. In this section, I have tried to include a few favourite dishes that have stood the test of time:

Potbread

1 packet (800 g) self-raising flour
1 teaspoon salt
2 teaspoons sugar
1 egg
1 teaspoon baking powder
2 tins beer (340 ml)
(For variation, add sunflower or other types of seeds, and oxtail or onion soup powder.)

Mix the ingredients together and knead thoroughly, working the dough through with your fingers. Mould the dough into a ball and place in an oiled, flat-bottomed iron pot that has been pre-heated. Let it stand near the fire in medium heat for 15 minutes. Make a round, flat hole about 50–70 millimetres wide in the soil and fill it with fresh, glowing coals. Allow the coals to heat up the hole for a few minutes, and then cover lightly with sand. Place the pot on top and then add a circle of embers around the base. These must not touch the pot, although you can put some glowing embers on top of the lid. If you see that the embers have become covered in ash, add new ones. Leave the pot for one hour. After 45 minutes, test the bread with a knife.

Vetkoek

This is delicious with butter and jam, or even with savoury mince.

3 cups flour
1 teaspoon baking powder
2 cups water or milk (powdered milk can also be used)
1 teaspoon salt
1 egg

Cooking oil
Butter, jam or savoury mince

Mix the flour, baking powder, water or milk and salt together and beat into a runny mixture. Beat the egg and add to the rest, mixing well. Heat a pot half full of cooking oil and put large spoonfuls of dough into the hot oil. Each spoonful will form a ball. Remove from the pot once the vetkoek are golden-brown, and put on a paper napkin to drain.

Veld Pudding

(Recipe courtesy of Mrs Y. du Plessis of Etosha):

2 cups flour
2 teaspoons ground ginger
2 tablespoons smooth apricot jam
2 teaspoons salt
2 teaspoons ground cinnamon
3 teaspoons bicarbonate of soda mixed with 1 cup of milk
3 tablespoons of mixed dried fruit and nuts
2 tablespoons margarine or butter
1 egg
5 cups water
2 cups brown sugar
2–3 cups dessert wine
Custard or cream

Mix together the flour, ginger, jam, salt, cinnamon, bicarbonate, dried fruit and nuts. Add the margarine or butter, and the beaten egg. Boil the water in a flat-bottomed iron pot, and add the brown sugar to form a syrup. Add spoonfuls of the mixture into the boiling syrup. Allow it to simmer for 30 minutes, then add the dessert wine. Serve with custard or cream. This is a wonderful treat, especially in winter.

Pineapple Fridge Tart

I suggest that you prepare this dish one evening ahead and leave it in the fridge overnight.

1 large tin pineapple pulp
1 tin condensed milk
2 tablespoons lemon juice
1 tablespoon gelatine
1 container cottage cheese
1 packet tennis biscuits

Mix the pineapple, condensed milk, lemon juice, gelatine and cottage cheese together. Pack some of the tennis biscuits on the bottom and sides of a Tupperware container and sprinkle with lemon juice. Pour in the mixture and add some crumbed tennis biscuits on the top. Leave the tart in the fridge to set.

10

SAFETY

A good fire extinguisher and a well-stocked first-aid kit are essential items of safety equipment on any off-road trip. By adhering to the following safety precautions, you can help prevent accidents from occurring:

• Keep all inflammable items (such as fuel and gas) at a safe distance from sources of electricity and your camp fire.

• Never use candles, gas or paraffin lamps inside a tent (*see* pages 93 and 110).

• Build your camp fire downwind, at a safe distance from the tents, vehicles or any flammable and explosive matter.

• Do not allow children to ride on roof carriers or spare wheels fixed to the vehicle's bonnet.

FIRE PREVENTION

You should be prepared in case a fire breaks out in your vehicle. This tends to happen unexpectedly, with the result that most people immediately panic. Take the following precautions:

• Keep a No. 13 spanner in the cabin within easy reach of the driver, so that he or she can quickly disconnect the battery terminals.

• Keep a fire extinguisher in the cabin within easy reach.

• Before going on the trip, hold a fire drill involving everybody who will be travelling in the vehicle.

• Do not smoke while refuelling your vehicle from a jerry can, and do not refuel close to the camp fire. Whenever you are refuelling, a member of the group should stand by with a fire extinguisher, safety pin removed and ready.

• If you are using PVC jerry cans, which I do not recommend (*see* page 47), each can must be brushed off with a damp cotton rag before refuelling in order to eliminate any static electricity.

• Before fuel is siphoned over from jerry cans, switch off gas-operated fridges and freezers – especially if the filler cap is near the fridge.

• Be careful when you are driving through long grass, as it tends to collect under the vehicle and can easily be ignited due to its proximity to the hot exhaust pipe. Construct a grating tool out of thick, strong, fencing wire (*bloudraad*). Stop the vehicle approximately every 15 minutes and make use of the grating tool to scratch out all the grass which has become packed in, near or around the manifold and exhaust pipe.

YOUR VEHICLE
• Have your vehicle thoroughly serviced before a trip to ensure that it is in excellent working order.

• Do not overload your vehicle or the roof carrier, as this alters the vehicle's centre of gravity and can make it less stable on inclines.

• Wear your safety belt and drive cautiously. Fast driving on a 4x4 route is dangerous.

• Never consume alcohol when driving in off-road conditions.

THE CAMP
• Never set up camp in the dark.

• Inspect your chosen camp site for scorpion holes, and for elephant and hippo footpaths.

• Ensure that your camp site has adequate lighting.

• Keep your tent closed, day and night, under all circumstances. Never be slack about this.

• Build the camp fire with short pieces of wood. Branches that stick out are easy to trip over.

• When you are cooking over an open fire, wear leather gloves to prevent burns.

• Maintain a high standard of hygiene at all times.

FINDING WATER

In the dry savanna regions of Southern Africa it is sometimes difficult to find water, particularly during the winter months when rain is scarce in the interior and water sources have dried up. Here are a few handy hints on where to look for water:

• As far as you can, try to plan your itinerary so that you travel between water points, especially if you are planning to go to the remote parts of Botswana and Namibia.

• Always carry enough water to survive for a week in case of an emergency. I once came across a group of people who had been stranded in Kaokoland for three days. Fortunately, they had broken down on the main route where vehicles pass through at least once a week, and had taken sufficient water to last them for the duration of their trip. However, this trip could easily have ended in tragedy if it had not been for the foresight of the tour leader.

• Most land surveyor maps indicate lakes, dams, pans, etc, but bear in mind that these water sources may be dry in winter, as it rains during the summer months in most parts of the interior of Southern Africa. Coastal areas of the Western Cape, however, are located in a winter rainfall area.

• In the Namib and Kalahari deserts, the presence of birds is a good indication of water. By noting the direction in which the birds are flying, you can steer your vehicle towards water. For example, the Namaqua sandgrouse (*Pterocles namaqua*) heads for water each morning and evening, sometimes flying distances of as much as 70 kilometres. However, in the dry savanna bush of the Kalahari you can drive for hours without seeing any birds (except for raptors). Suddenly, you will come across an abundance of different birds – a sure sign that there is water located within a 10-kilometre radius.

• Antelope tracks and a higher concentration of dung are another good indication that water can be found nearby.

• Riverbeds are always a source of water. I have seen Himba people digging wells of up to four or five metres deep in the dry riverbeds of Kaokoland. Elephant, with their keen sense of smell, are also able to open up 'gorras' with their feet. Follow the riverbed to where it makes a sharp turn against a bank or rock face. These obstacles store water for many months, and a couple of metres' digging should soon reveal water.

• If you are absolutely desperate, you will have to drink your vehicle's radiator water. However, I do not recommend this, as the water contains a lot of metal which could upset your stomach and even poison you.

• You could also try an old army trick: make a round hole about 30–50 centimetres deep in the ground. Put some squashed green vegetation inside the hole and place a container in the middle. Cover the hole with a plastic sheet and put a stone on top of the sheet in the centre. Water will soon rise out of the vegetation and condense on the underside of the plastic sheet.

The stone will create a funnel in the sheet and, drop by drop, the container will fill up with water.

• Use every opportunity that you have to refill your water containers.

INSECTS

• Always wear boots or shoes with a high ankle, and wear socks in the evenings. Special precautions should be taken in malaria-infested areas, such as wearing long trousers and long-sleeved shirts in the evenings (*see* page 104).

• Don't wear blue- or white-coloured clothes in tsetse fly country, as these colours attract the flies. In general, brightly-coloured clothing is not recommended.

• Use insect repellent liberally.

WILDLIFE

• Always keep a safe distance from wild animals, especially breeding herds of elephant.

• Do not stop at a camp site with the car windows open. In many areas, baboons and monkeys have become a nuisance as a result of people feeding them. Monkeys are so sly that they will jump through the window the moment you stop, and run off with something before you can react. Baboons will attack you to get to your food. To drive them off, take along a catapult and a bag full of stones (there may be no stones on the ground); a few well-placed shots should convince them to depart. To prevent them tearing your tents apart in search of food, place a few rubber snakes on the tents to scare them. Above all, do not feed these animals.

STAYING IN TOUCH

• Before you leave, give a copy of your detailed itinerary to a friend. On a regular basis, let him or her know how you are progressing.

• A long-distance, high-frequency radiotelephone is a very useful device to have on any off-roading trip (*see* page 51). If you break down or run into trouble, you can quickly notify the relevant people.

• Always be prepared in case of an emergency. Before departing, find out which rescue services operate in the areas that you intend visiting, and investigate where you will be able to find help if you break down.

• If someone requires urgent medical attention or evacuation, you may need to contact a medical rescue service. There are many such organisations in Southern Africa, and it is worthwhile to have contact details handy in case of emergency.

11

HYGIENE AND FIRST AID

Any extended off-road trip will naturally carry with it a risk of illness, and seems to attract all the nasties in the bacteria world. To reduce the possibility of anyone becoming ill, take the following basic precautions:

• Regularly add Milton or Jik to the scullery water, and do not leave the washing-up for the next day.

• Thoroughly disinfect the cooler box and/or fridge/freezer before going on the trip.

• Always disinfect your drinking water (use Milton liquid or special purification tablets). Boil the water if you do not have any chemical aids or if the water simply tastes awful. There are several very effective water purifiers available on the market, and some are even equipped with 12-volt pumps which can be installed in the vehicle. These units are very useful aids.

• When you are using the bush for your ablutions, do not leave the toilet paper uncovered. Always make a hole about 10 centimetres deep in the soil and cover it when you are finished. This so-called 'cat method' will help the naturally occurring bacteria in the soil to break down your waste matter into useful compost.

• Wash your hands regularly and keep your fingernails and toenails short and clean.

• If possible, you should shower or wash every day. Always wash your posterior before going to bed as the sweating produced from sitting for long periods in the hot car can easily cause a painful fungal infection to develop.

Common ailments

Through the years, I've found that there are four ailments or mishaps which occur most regularly on safari. These are listed below, together with some simple remedies and treatments:

1. *Constipation:* Dried fruit, and especially prunes, works wonders.
2. *Diarrhoea:* Flat Coca-Cola, black tea, white bread and, of course, Immodium.
3. *Burns on the hands:* Spray with Solarcaine, apply a petroleum-gel gauze and bind with a clean bandage.
4. *Cuts:* Clean immediately with Mercurochrome, apply an antiseptic ointment, put cotton gauze on top and bandage.

• Keep some Wet Ones or scented napkins in the vehicle. They are wonderful to use for cleaning, freshening up or for when you have finished your ablutions.

• Avoid taking white meats (chicken, fish, pork and veal) on a tour, unless they are frozen solid – try to cook them first. White meats are highly susceptible to salmonella infection, which causes severe diarrhoea and even food poisoning (*see* page 113). Exceptions to this are smoked pork (Kassler) and cured bacon, which last quite a long time if kept cool.

• The amenities in some reserves and national parks, especially in Botswana, are very dirty. Always wear sandals in the shower, and clean the toilet seat before sitting.

• Indigenous people with infections, burns or lacerations will often wander into your camp. Always wear surgical gloves when treating somebody, even if it is a member of your own group.

THE FIRST-AID KIT

If you are travelling in a group, at least one person on the tour should have formal training in first aid. In fact, it is advisable for any off-road enthusiast to follow one of the first-aid courses that are offered through organisations such as the South African Red Cross Society or the St. John Ambulance.

Before you leave, ask your doctor to advise you which medicines you should take along. This is important if you are taking any prescribed drugs or are allergic to sulpha and other medicines. Inform the tour leader, or the person responsible for first aid, of any conditions that you suffer from, especially if you are a diabetic or have heart problems.

Ready for an emergency

The first-aid kit should contain at least the following items:

- Anti-emetic
  (*prevents nausea and vomiting*)
- Antispasmodic
  (*prevents stomach cramps*)
- Prescription painkillers
- Antihistamine tablets and
  ointment
  (*treats insect bites and allergies*)
- Antibiotics
  (*specifics or broad-spectrum*)
- Fungicide ointment
  (*destroys fungi*)
- Medicine for diarrhoea
- Medicine for constipation
- Petroleum-gel gauze
  (*for minor wounds and burns*)
- Antiseptic fluid and salve
- Adrenaline inhalant or injection
  against bee-sting allergies
- Local anaesthetic spray
- Eye wash and drops
- Malaria prophylaxis
- Thermometer
- Snake bite kit
  (*get the syringe-sucking type*)
- Scorpion sting and spider
  bite spray
- Plasters, bandages and
  cotton wool
- Splints
- Anti-dehydration compound
  (*added to water; replaces salts
  and minerals lost through
  perspiration*)
- Cold, 'flu and sinus tablets
- Surgical gloves
- Scissors
- Tweezers

Bad spirits

Once I was stopped by a Himba man, whose hut was next to the road, and who complained of constipation. As we were in a hurry, I handed him a small bottle of Brooklax. In our haste, my assistant did not translate my instructions correctly. Three days later, we passed the same way, but at a more relaxed pace. We stopped, and found my 'stomach friend' sitting in the sun against his hut. His face was grey, but he radiated a serene happiness. When I questioned him, he explained that he had drunk the whole bottle in one sitting. He was firmly convinced that all the 'bad spirits' had now left his body. I treated him for dehydration, and this time made sure he clearly understood my instructions.

12

THE HUMAN ELEMENT

The success of any off-road tour is determined by the people involved. You may have the best vehicles, equipment and maps available, and plan your journey meticulously, but, if there is discord among the group members, you will not have an enjoyable experience.

Most groups head for the bush in a festive mood – an adventure lies ahead and everyone is on holiday. However, we tend to forget that each of us has fears and insecurities which can emerge under certain conditions. After spending an arduous day in the bush, most people are usually hungry, tired and irritable. Some individuals could feel isolated from the rest of the group, and others could have fears that previously went unnoticed. There are two things that intensify conflict between people: one is a lack of leadership, the other a lack of specified functions.

Whenever organised groups of people have journeyed into unknown territory, such as the Great Trek of 1836, they have formed themselves into an organised unit, with clear divisions of responsibility. Although the days of trekking in ox-wagons are gone, such migrations have lessons for us even today. A kommandant (tour leader) generally headed up a large group of people, whose members each performed specified tasks in accordance with their knowledge and experience: for instance, there were butchers, mechanics and cobblers. The men attended to the wagons and the oxen, while the women saw to the food, medicine and hygiene.

A convoy of off-roaders should operate in much the same way. Stand together and help one another, particularly when faced with a crisis. I once observed members of a group jeering and mocking a teammate because his vehicle had got stuck. This behaviour adversely affects the morale of the group. Therefore, if you intend travelling in a group, bear the following advice in mind:

• Elect a tour leader. This person should be chosen by consensus, and everybody in the group should respect his or her authority while on the tour.

• The leader should be responsible for organisation and co-ordination of the tour, and should use consensus as far as possible when making important decisions.

• Each person in the group should be responsible for a specific task. For instance, somebody acts as the medic, another the mechanic and someone else the cook. When preparing for the tour, it is the duty of each person to submit lists of equipment to the tour leader. The lists serve as a basis for discussion of what needs to be taken on the tour. In this way, the group will avoid taking too much (or too little) into the bush. The following is a shortlist of suggested functions:

- The tour leader
- The navigator
- The mechanic
- The cook
- The loadmaster
- The barman
- The musician
- The pastor
- The treasurer
- The campmaster

• Draw up a timetable for all the chores that need to be done so that nobody can shirk tedious tasks. A chore list is a sure way to negate the possibility of group conflict erupting. It is also very important that nobody escapes having to do chores.

• A group should consist of more than three people, but no more than ten (including children). If the group is too big, there will be no cohesion, and sub-groups, each with their own subculture (e.g., private jokes and leaders), could start to develop. A large group is also more difficult to cater for, organise and co-ordinate. After all, the trip should not be a taxing exercise, but a time of enjoyment and relaxation.

• Undisciplined children can cause serious conflict between people on a tour. Children on a tour must be well behaved, as they could otherwise expose themselves and others to danger.

• A tour into an untamed, wild or unknown area should consist of a minimum of two vehicles, but not more than five. Apart from the dust that is raised by five vehicles, the convoy becomes too drawn-out, and the people in the last vehicle miss out on sightings. To prevent this from happening, the last vehicle (the *agteros*) should be given the opportunity to shift to the front (to be the *voorbok*) at intervals, with the *voorbok* becoming second in line. However, if special knowledge of a route is required, or if the *voorbok* has a GPS and was given the task of leading the convoy, he or she must remain in first position and the second vehicle must move to the back of the line.

• I strongly recommend that you use two-way short-distance FM mobile radios to communicate between vehicles (*see* page 52). Not only can the *voorbok* then warn the others if vehicles are approaching or if there is an animal in the road, but he or she can also pass on information about the wildlife and other interesting sights. If a vehicle down the line develops a problem, you can also use the two-way radio to inform the rest of the group. This easy communication adds to group cohesion, safety and shared enjoyment of the tour.

BUSH CHARACTERS

Let me also warn you about two characters who tend to emerge while on tour. My observations are borne out by years of experience:

• Stressful Sam: He gets very worked up if the route becomes uncertain to the navigator and tries to bully everyone into following his route. Sam must be told in no uncertain terms that he is not the navigator. Of course, Sam is going to throw a tantrum. He will start sulking and may even pack his things and leave the group. Do not concern yourself with him.

• Moaning Mary: She is either too hot, or too cold, and complains constantly about the dust and the

Phobia

We were heading for the deep-dune Namib Desert behind Walvis Bay and planned to emerge from the wilderness three days later at Sossusvlei. Our proposed route would take us over some of the highest dunes in the world, so the Land Rover stayed in diff-lock for the whole journey. My companions on the trip were a Nature Conservation colleague and a doctor from Windhoek. There were three vehicles making up the convoy, with the Chief Warden of the Namib–Naukluft Park in the lead. My colleague insisted on driving my vehicle. Halfway up the first dune, to my great dismay, he stalled. Before I could say anything to him, he jumped out the door and ran away.

With great difficulty, I reversed my vehicle and tried to climb the dune again. Meanwhile, my doctor friend got out and went over to my colleague. I was so busy with the ascent and descent that I did not give them any further attention until I had cleared the dune.

After successfully descending the dune, I stopped for a cigarette in the 'street' – the depression between two dunes – to wait for my companions to catch up. I was greatly astonished to see my doctor friend helping my colleague over the edge of the dune, with my colleague creeping on all fours and crying like a baby. When they reached me, I called the doctor to one side, very disturbed by this incident. He told me my colleague was suffering from a fear of heights in its worst form. What could we do? There were two-and-a-half days still ahead and there was no way we could turn back.

In the end, we injected our friend with a sedative and gave him a glass of neat whisky, which knocked him out. We bound him to the front seat with ropes, so that only his head swayed as we navigated the dunes. In the evening, we were dog-tired, but our friend, having slept the whole day, wanted to party. It was with considerable relief that we reached the 'Dead Vlei' at Sossus at lunchtime on the third day. Our experience showed me that human frailties are never far from the surface – especially out in the wilderness.

flies. There is not enough water for her shampoo. Somewhere down the line, she develops a sore back and can hardly lift her hands to help.

Mary is looking for attention, and likes to manipulate people. Ignore her, and she will suddenly and miraculously be healed.

13

BUSH ETIQUETTE

Bush etiquette can be divided into do's and don'ts. Everyone has a responsibility to treat the environment and local residents with respect and courtesy.

THE DO'S

• Be friendly and polite at all check-points and frontier posts. Respect the authority of the officials on duty.

• Familiarise yourself with rules and regulations of any conservation areas through which you will be passing. Adhere to those rules.

• Camp only in designated sites, unless for some reason (breakdown or emergency) this is impossible.

• Before camping near an African homestead, always ask the permission of the inhabitants. If some form of remuneration is required, then you should pay it.

• Never walk into an African homestead without first obtaining permission. Wait outside the enclosure until somebody comes to investigate, and then ask for permission to enter. Ask this person to act as a guide, as unknown circumstances or conditions may exist which you may disturb. Although you may be curious about their lifestyle, do not enter or peer into their houses. The residents have the same right to privacy which you enjoy in your own home.

• Many African people like to visit travellers at their campsite. This is their way of welcoming you to their neighbourhood. They may like to sit at the fire for a while, as fire plays a central role in their commu-nity as a symbol of hospitality. Do not offer them alcohol; rather give them a cool drink and some food as a token of thanks and hospitality.

• Be aware of cultural differences when meeting indigenous people. For instance, do not play rap music and expect a Himba girl to dance with you. African people dance for different reasons from Western people. Do not give them presents that they cannot use – if you wish to give them something, offer them sugar or mealie meal.

• Do not cheat people when buying artefacts and souvenirs, or try to buy something that is not being offered for sale: some items, such as the conch shells worn by Himba women, are heirlooms passed down from mother to daughter.

• Always ask people if you may take photographs of them. If they would like payment, oblige them.

• Use firewood sparingly. I find it shocking how some groups misuse firewood. In Botswana and Namibia, I have observed people using 4x4 vehicles and chains to uproot trees to make their fires! These types of people need to become aware of the damage they are doing to the environment. In the desolate Namib and Kalahari deserts, you should not gather firewood at all, but should take your own charcoal or firewood.

• Ask the owner's permission before you enter, or camp on, a farm or any enclosed property.

• If you open a gate, close it once you have passed through.

• Wherever possible, ask permission before you take any water from a well or pump.

• Rowdiness should not be allowed in the camp after 10:00 p.m. Remember that everyone needs a good night's rest after a full day.

• Do not leave your car alarm on at night as it could go off and disturb everyone's sleep.

• Leave only your tracks when departing from a camp site.

• Report poachers, hoodlums and rowdy people to the authorities.

THE DON'TS

• Don't camp near a water source. Camp at least three kilometres away (*see* page 105).

• Don't use soap or shampoo if you are washing in a river or stream. Fill a bucket with water instead, and find a place away from the water source to wash yourself.

• Don't leave any toilet paper uncovered. Use the 'cat' method and bury all the evidence.

• Don't leave your refuse behind or try to bury it, as scavengers will dig it up. Keep refuse in a sturdy bag and wait until you reach a town or an official municipal dump before disposing of it (*see* page 103).

• Don't make fires against trees or leave fires burning when departing your camp site (*see* page 109).

• Don't dish out money or other items to the beggars who some-times congregate at fuel stops. Sometimes a handout to one produces a riotous free-for-all, with a shower of stones hurled at your vehicle as you flee the scene.

• Don't take fruit into Botswana's game reserves or into some Zimbabwean parks, such as Mana Pools. In Botswana, you are

prohibited from taking fruit into the game reserves, as elephants have a keen sense of smell and will destroy your food boxes (and even your vehicle) if they smell fruit.

• Don't approach wild animals even if they look peaceful.

• Don't try to handle tame-looking animals, such as mongoose and suricate, as they could have rabies.

• Don't imitate the Camel Trophy teams. Drive slowly and stay alert.

• Don't under any circumstances make new tracks in sensitive areas such as the gravel plains of the Namib Desert (*see* page 63). If the road is washboarded, deflate your vehicle's tyres and proceed slowly.

• Don't make a noise at water holes. Sit quietly and be patient. You will be rewarded.

• Don't throw a burning cigarette away as it could cause a serious veld fire. Smokers should never discard their cigarette butts in the veld, but should use a tin as an ashtray.

• Don't throw your leftover food into the bush. Put it in a refuse bag and hang the bag high above the ground at night.

• Don't feed jackal, hyaena, baboon, monkey, warthog or any other wild animals.

In recent years, I have noted the increasingly aggressive behaviour of baboon, monkey and hyaena in the parks of Botswana and northern Zimbabwe. There are a number of reasons for this, but the main one is that people feed these animals.

At Savuti in the Chobe National Park, I have seen hyaena walk right into the circle of firelight, having lost their fear of fire, while people threw leftover braai meat at them in order to take a good photograph.

At Serondella in the Chobe and at Third Bridge in Botswana's

Moremi National Park, I saw people feeding sweets to monkeys and baboons, which led to a troop of baboons attacking a camp site.

Complaints to the authorities in Botswana seem to lead nowhere, but in Zimbabwe the game wardens are taking drastic (and deadly) measures to keep these animals under control. At Okaukuejo in the Etosha National Park, jackal will steal meat directly from the grill, even though the camps in Namibia are fenced in (they dig holes under the fencing). The authorities here regularly shoot these animals to prevent them from becoming a nuisance. Remember that wild animals that have lost their fear of humans are dangerous, and have to be killed. Do not unwittingly sentence these animals to death by feeding them.

CHECKLISTS

CHECKLIST FOR CAMPING GEAR

Tents	☐	Tables/table cloth	☐
Tent poles/struts	☐	Lights (electric)	☐
Tent pegs	☐	Gas lamps and wicks	☐
Fly sheets	☐	Gas bottle	☐
Bungee cords	☐	Gas regulator and pipes	☐
Stretchers	☐	Primus stove	☐
Sleeping rolls	☐	Gas cooking rings	☐
Sheets	☐	Gas rubber hose	☐
Blankets	☐	Gas rubber hose-clamps/venturis	☐
Cushions	☐	Tarpaulin	☐
Sleeping bags	☐	Rope/Tie-downs	☐
Mattresses	☐	Wire (draad)	☐
Tent lamp	☐	Axe	☐
Torch	☐	Spade	☐
Batteries	☐	Potjie box	☐
Chairs	☐	Pots and pans	☐

Kettle	☐	Crockery containers	☐
Grill	☐	Cutlery boxes/containers	☐
Grill stands	☐	Toilet	☐
Leather gloves (for use when cooking over a grill)	☐	Toilet paper	☐
		Hand wash stand	☐
Fire lighters	☐	Scullery	☐
Lighter/matches	☐	Scullery detergent/soap	☐
Shower	☐	Drying/washing towels	☐
Shower curtain	☐	Laundry soap/pegs	☐
Shower floor (black PVC blocks)	☐	Insect repellent and coils	☐
Water cans/containers/ buckets	☐	Mosquito nets	☐
		Water purifying tablets	☐
Fridge/freezer	☐	Milton liquid (or Jik)	☐
Fridge fuses	☐	Canvas water bags	☐
Fridge spare socket	☐	Cool drinks	☐
Cooler box	☐	Alcoholic beverages	☐
First-aid box	☐	Generator/lead	☐
Food boxes/containers	☐	Thermos flasks	☐

CHECKLIST FOR VEHICLE PARTS

Fuel pump	☐	Coil	☐
Fanbelt (x 2)	☐	Fuses (several)	☐
Front and back shock absorber	☐	Fuel filter	☐
		Fuel line	☐
Points	☐	Clamps (different sizes)	☐
Condenser	☐	Spare wheel	☐
Spark plugs	☐	Isolation tape	☐

Indian Cement (or Bar's Leaks) ☐	Inner tube ☐
Gasket maker ☐	Loosening oil ☐
Gun gum ☐	Patch and solution ☐
Fuel tank repair gum ☐	Gator and gator awl ☐
Radiator hose and clamps ☐	Tyre valve and tool ☐
Rear/front light bulbs ☐	Tyre pressure gauge ☐
Clutch and brake fluid ☐	Hose for jerry cans ☐
Engine oil ☐	Bloudraad ☐
Transfer case/gear box oil ☐	Bindraad ☐
Differential oil ☐	Jerry cans ☐
Automatic gear oil/hydraulic	Tow rope ☐
steering fluid ☐	Fire extinguisher ☐

CHECKLIST FOR TOOLS

Hi-lift jack ☐	Hacksaw ☐
Bottle jack ☐	Shifting spanner ☐
Wheel spanner ☐	Jumper leads ☐
Power bar ☐	Cordless drill and bits ☐
Tyre levers (x 3) ☐	Screws (self-tapering) ☐
Full set of spanners (inc. No. 13) ☐	Nuts and bolts (different sizes) ☐
Screwdrivers ☐	Pop-rivet gun & rivets ☐
Pliers ☐	Tyre pump ☐
Hammer and rubber hammer ☐	Allen keys ☐
Vice grip ☐	Timber for use as jacking plate ☐

PERSONAL CHECKLIST

Suitcase and clothes	☐	ID/Passport (inc. visas)	☐
Toilet bag	☐	Money	☐
Warm jacket	☐	Credit card	☐
Shoes/strops	☐	Petrol card	☐
Prescribed medicine	☐	Travellers' cheques	☐
Cap/hat	☐	Travel itinerary	☐
Dark glasses	☐	Address book	☐
Sunblock	☐	Calculator	☐
Binoculars	☐	Camera/lenses/film	☐
Pocket knife	☐	Video camcorder	☐
Bird book	☐	Cassettes	☐
GPS	☐	Batteries/penlite	☐
Plant book	☐	Music cassettes	☐
Note pad	☐	Lighter	☐
Pen	☐	Cigarettes/ashtray (if a smoker!)	☐
Wallet	☐	Maps/ruler	☐
Driver's licence	☐	Reading material	☐

GLOSSARY

Aardvark (*Orycteropus afer*): (Proto-Afrikaans) A nocturnal burrowing African mammal that has long ears and snout and feeds on termites. In modern Afrikaans – 'erdvark'.

Agteros: (Afrikaans) The last or slowest ox, or even 'slowpoke'.

Baboon spider: A large, hairy (but fortunately harmless) spider known in Afrikaans as *bobejaan-spinnekop*.

Bakkie: (Afrikaans) A pick-up truck. Afrikaans from the American-English word 'buggy', meaning a horse-drawn passenger vehicle.

Bindraad: a soft fencing wire.

Bloudraad: (Afrikaans) A thick, very strong, galvanised fencing wire which is not easily bent or broken.

Braai: (Afrikaans) A barbecue, shortening of *braaivleis*, which means 'roasted meat'.

Bundu: (Swahili) The wild bush or unmapped areas of the African savanna.

Fat tackies: (South African) Slang for wide off-road tyres.

Gorra: (Khoikhoi) A water hole, usually dug by an elephant.

Himba: A Hamitic Bantu-speaking tribe of Herero-speaking people living in Kaokoland, Namibia. Directly translated, 'Himba' means 'beggar'.

Kalahari: Extensive desert and sand system stretching from South Africa to the southern Congo.

Laager: (Proto-Afrikaans) A circle formed for protection or defence by ox-wagons on trek.

Marie biscuits: A humorous South African reference to narrow tyres. Marie biscuits are a well-known type of biscuit enjoyed with tea.

Mealie meal: (South African) Maize meal used for cooking. Also known as *sadza* in Zimbabwe and Zambia, and *mieliepap* in South Africa and Namibia.

Middelmannetjie: (Afrikaans) The 'small middle man', or the area between the tracks of vehicles.

Namib: The world's oldest desert, situated on the west coast of Namibia, between Angola and the Olifants River in South Africa.

Potjie: (Afrikaans) A three-legged cast-iron cooking pot (of various sizes) used over an open fire.

Riempiestoel: (Afrikaans) A chair with a seat (and/or back) woven from strips of animal hide.

Skottelbraai: Originally a shallow pan fashioned from a plough; nowadays purpose-made for use with camping gas bottles.

Spoor: (Afrikaans) The track of an animal, person, or vehicle. To spoor: when a vehicle follows in the tracks left by the preceding vehicle.

Trek: (Afrikaans) A long and often difficult journey, especially a migration by ox-wagon.

Veld: (Afrikaans) Savanna, open grassland or bush.

Vetkoek: (Afrikaans) Deep-fried dough balls, sometimes eaten with jam or savoury mince.

Voorbok: (Afrikaans) The leading goat or leader of the party, or even a petulant person.

Index

Page numbers in **bold** refer to main entries; those in *italics* refer to photographs or illustrations.

Index

PHOTOGRAPHIC CREDITS

front cover: Jean du Plessis (main pic); front cover left column: John Haigh (all); back cover: Chanan Weiss; spine: Roger de la Harpe/Struik Image Library; title page: Johan Kloppers; p. 65, pp. 66–67 top: Jean du Plessis; p. 66 bottom left: Patrick Wagner/Getaway/Photo Access; p. 67 bottom right: Jean du Plessis; pp. 68–69: Chanan Weiss; p. 70: Patrick Wagner/Getaway/Photo Access; p. 71 top: David Rogers/Getaway/Photo Access; p. 71 bottom: Patrick Wagner/Getaway/Photo Access; pp. 72–73: David Rogers/Getaway/Photo Access; p. 74: Johan Kloppers; p. 75 top: Chanan Weiss; p. 75 bottom: David Rogers/Getaway/Photo Access; pp. 76–77, p. 78 top: Johan Kloppers; p. 78 bottom: Jean du Plessis; p. 79: Johan Kloppers; p. 80: Don Pinnock/Getaway/Photo Access.

ACKNOWLEDGEMENTS

I would like to extend my thanks to Elizabeth Duke, of Windhoek, for patiently typing the manuscript and subsequent revisions, and to my sister, Paula Joubert, for her help with the initial sketches for the illustrations. Further, I wish to thank the whole team at Struik Publishers, especially managing editor Annlerie van Rooyen and editor Alfred LeMaitre, without whose support and patient advice this project would never have seen the light of day. Design manager Janice Evans and designers Sonia Hedenskog-de Villiers and Dominic Robson worked extremely hard under tight deadlines to produce the design. I thank my wife Charlotte, for her constant encouragement and the Joubert clan, for their support. Finally, I thank God, who gave me the insight and the love of His creation – and the strength to finish.

The publishers wish to thank the staff of the AA Auto Shop, Cape Town, for their kind assistance in the production of the cover.